STEPMOTHER

STEPMOTHER

Redeeming a Disdained Vocation

Dorothy C. Bass

BROADLEAF BOOKS
MINNEAPOLIS

STEPMOTHER
Redeeming a Disdained Vocation

Unless otherwise noted, Scripture quotations are from the New
Revised Standard Version Bible, copyright © 1989 National Council
of the Churches of Christ in the United States of America. Used by
permission. All rights reserved worldwide.

Psalm 148 from *Evangelical Lutheran Worship*, copyright © 2006
Evangelical Lutheran Church in America admin. Augsburg Fortress.

Cover image: © Adobe Stock 2021; Continuous one line drawing by
Valenty and © iStock 2021; White wood texture by Zocha_K
Cover design: 1517 Media

Print ISBN: 978-1-5064-7867-8
eBook ISBN: 978-1-5064-7868-5

Printed in Canada

To my stepdaughter, her mother, and her father

CONTENTS

1

OUT OF THE SHADOWS

I am sitting in an Adirondack chair made of spruce from the forest that presses in on this alpine village from every side. Mark and I have come from Chicago to this, his favorite place in the world, for our honeymoon. Today he's out hiking, his fly rod in hand. He'll be back soon, almost certainly with a few rainbow trout for tomorrow's breakfast.

On my lap is Mark's only child, and on her lap is the book that has become our favorite in the four days since we arrived. Kristen is almost five years old. In this moment, I can think of nothing I'd rather do than read this book to this lively, imaginative child. She leans forward into the tale of Molly Whuppie, glancing up at me in knowing amusement whenever the overconfident giant sets another of his nefarious schemes in motion. At last, by wit and courage, Molly defeats him for good. Satisfied, Kristen and I lie back onto the warm, fragrant wood. I tilt my head to rest my cheek against her braided yellow hair, and our breathing falls into a shared rhythm, each breath longer than the last. This lapful of child, this communion with a little one for whom I already feel overwhelming love, brings a joy I've been seeking for years. I am at peace, and I can feel in the looseness of her limbs that she is too.

But we are not alone.

A white-haired gentleman, whom I have so far failed to notice, has been listening in on the story from a few yards away. When he spots an opening, he catches Kristen's eye, smiles, and speaks to her in a grandfatherly way.

"I see that you and your mommy are both wearing the same T-shirt!" he says.

Hearing *mommy*, Kristen bolts upright and turns to me with a look of confusion and distress. Her mommy is hundreds of miles away. What is this man talking about? Our breathing quickens and diverges, and my joy shatters into pieces. I do not want to speak to this man. I try to will him away. But Kristen has been addressed, and she has turned to me for help, so I must answer for us both.

"I'm not her mother," I say. "I'm her stepmother."

As soon as I utter this ugly word, everything changes. Now her look is one of alarm.

"You are not my stepmother!" she cries. I can tell that stories she has heard are flashing through her mind. Stepmothers are wicked! Stepmothers are mean to little girls and boys! I try to comfort her, but I cannot say, "Of course, honey, you're right; I'm not your stepmother." All I can do is whisper, "Shh, shh, everything is okay" while I gather her again into my lap. She is not persuaded. Sobbing, she hides her face in my shoulder while I pat her back. I desperately wish that Mark would return to show her his catch and turn this day in a new direction.

It soon becomes obvious that the white-haired gentleman is also distressed. He never intended to upset this child, and he is deeply sorry to have made her cry. His eyes downcast, he mumbles an apology and walks away. His sorrowful demeanor, I suspect, reflects a deeper concern as well: he is sad that a child so young has had to endure the breakup of her original home. He does not say this, but this is what I think I glimpse in his face, perhaps because I have suddenly had that same thought. How sad for Kristen that her parents have divorced. Caught up in my own new love, I have papered over the loss suffered by this little girl.

I've been kidding myself, I realize. I don't belong here, in this chair, with this book, holding this child. Kristen should be not on my lap but on the lap of her mother, the woman who gave her birth, the woman with whom she has previously traveled to this place. An aunt, teacher, or babysitter might be acceptable as a temporary substitute, I suppose. But not a stepmother—a woman whose very presence proves that Kristen's young life has already been marred by grief. A woman who is possibly a home-wrecker, probably a witch, and surely an interloper. A woman in whose body the terrible truth that families are fragile takes on flesh.

In the thirty-some years since that summer day, I've experienced the joy, sorrow, and confusion of stepmothering countless times. Happily, joy has come most often—but I'm pretty sure joy could surface only alongside acknowledgment that confusion and sorrow have also been present. The confusion is fueled in part by long-standing cultural images of stepmothers, of course. But confusion has also arisen in my own heart, as fantasies of maternal fulfillment implode, as strangers make assumptions about my marriage, and as I try to figure out where I fit in the life of someone I love and often care for in mother-like ways, but whose mother I am not.

And sorrow? A peaceful summer afternoon can come all too easily to an abrupt and tearful end. Those of us who choose partners who are parents step into relationships with children and adults already impacted by loss—and, importantly, loss within the very part of life we now share with them. Someone has died. Someone has divorced. Those who will come to be among our closest kin have been plunged into grief before we ever show up. Their stories are many and diverse, and in more than a few cases, the end of whatever came before was a good thing; divorce can bring liberation from terrible situations, and I remain grateful, for myself and others, that divorce is an option. Still, I can't shake the conviction that the world would be a better place if families didn't have wrenching schisms. In such a world, there would be no kids shuttling back and forth, no tense relationships between a first spouse and a second. But that is not the world in which we live.

In some imagined world where neither persons nor marriages die, there are no stepmothers. In the real world, stepmothers are everywhere, with hundreds of thousands of new stepmothers added to the tally each year in the United States alone. This sole statistic offers a glimpse into how fluid families are today and how rapidly they are changing, where one-third of all American children under eighteen are or have been part of a stepfamily, and 42 percent of all American adults have at least one close steprelative.

Yet how we understand our hopes and duties as family members has not kept pace with reality.

* * *

Each stepfamily has its own story. At the same time, the simple fact that there are so many stepfamilies demonstrates a shift in how Americans do family in the twenty-first century. We who long for love and connection even after loss, we who yearn for reliable companions for ourselves and our children in a time when so many things are unstable, we who strive to create a new family after the first one has fallen apart—we are developing a form of family life that is being woven into the fabric of our society. This form of family life provides a pattern of belonging for millions of individuals of every age. Questions about what this new form means and how it works confront us at every turn. But here we are. And it's along this path that we hope to find love, sustenance, and joy.

As our families walk this path, we stepmothers occupy a position that is crucial—crucial, meaning immensely important. Some books claim to tell you how to smooth everyone's journey and assure a fabulous outcome—which I too hope for and often see. But I also see our situation as surprisingly complicated, for stepmothers are well positioned to do harm as well as good. A stepmother is a stranger who has gained entry into the domestic world of a child. She may or may not be interested in developing a good relationship with the child or even in supporting the preexisting relationship between her partner and the child. She may compete with her stepchildren for their parent's time and resources or allow her own children to do so. The worries underlying negative stereotypes of stepmothers are sometimes well founded.

Just as a stepmother can hurt others, so too can she be hurt, by anything from outright rejection to feeling marginalized as other, more privileged caregivers set the schedules that shape her time. Thus stepmothers occupy a position that is crucial in another sense as well—crucial, meaning shaped like a cross, a site of suffering. Indeed, life on this cross may require a death of some kind. Perhaps jealousy will need to die, or resentment, or self-doubt, or fantasies about how things are supposed to be. Such emotions, even if well founded, can prevent us from recognizing the new life that is actually on offer in our stepfamilies.

When those of us who become stepmothers make a commitment to a new partner, we bring with us hopes as high, needs as great, and love as strong as those that accompany anyone else's leap into life together. But the terrain onto which we leap is strewn with hazards that are both material and spiritual. Being a stepmother is hard work, and we are unlikely to come through our labors unchanged.

Some of our work will be done in the neighborhood, the kitchen, or the car. But the bulk of our work—the most important part—will need to be done within our own hearts.

Being a stepmother is a complicated and demanding calling. For many of us, it's the hardest thing we've ever done; for all of us, it's among the most important. How we respond matters to the people we love and to us.

What might it mean to embrace this difficult calling wisely and well?

The first step is to bring stepmothers out of the shadows.

One famous stepmother, the widow of Snow White's father, revels in shadows. She lives in a castle by day, but when night falls she descends into a dark cellar. Transformed from beauty to hag, she prepares poison, not nourishment, for the youngster she ought to be protecting. An image of this horrid woman—the villain in Walt Disney's first feature film—sticks in the popular mind, along with a bevy of others like her. As Kristen's mother, Bekka, wrote to me in an email, "*Stepmother* has only one adjective that can precede it. *Wicked*. Well, maybe two. *Wicked* or *evil*." (Bekka is a stepmother too. We were commiserating about this widely held image.)

Even those of us who lack access to the dark arts often find that we have been cast into shadows conjured by moral judgment. While Americans are becoming more open to a range of family forms, patterns that disrupt the lives of children continue to be suspect. Preferring family constancy is understandable, but looking with disdain on individuals who are trying to adapt to unfamiliar circumstances is not. The shadow of judgment was cast on me in the course of my relatively fortunate daily life, and other stepmothers say they've felt that shadow too.

Disclosing that the child assumed to be mine is actually my stepchild leads onto complicated terrain, and not only with white-haired gentlemen. I remember the first time Mark and I took Kristen to the church we had recently joined. "Oh, I didn't know you have a child!" a woman remarked—catapulting me right back into that Adirondack chair in the mountains. My reply—"She's my stepdaughter"—caused the woman to mutter something vague and turn away as if she didn't know what to say next. For years I avoided mentioning our situation to people we did not know well, both to keep things simple and to protect myself from looks that seemed to range from disappointment to hostility.

All of us in our humanness have probably earned our share of the distrust stepmothers attract. We are no better than other people, other parents, other women. But taken as a group we are not any worse. And dispelling the shadows of distrust, disappointment, and disdain requires a gentle and generous approach, with others and ourselves. We'll need to come to terms with the thoughts and emotions that sometimes cause us to lose sleep or lash out. And we'll need to open our eyes to the light that sometimes breaks through the shadows, beaming love into our stepmotherly hearts.

Invisibility is a shadow of a different kind. We are absent from pictures of the baby coming home from the hospital. We cannot host the birthday party or sign the school forms. We may not be welcome at the wedding. Yet we are tied to our stepchildren in an intimate bond that has us performing something like motherhood for sizable portions of each year.

When we resent our stepchildren, it feels like all eyes are upon us. When we love them like crazy, we often have to do our loving from the sidelines.

Stepmothers are often the least visible members of stepfamilies. Researchers have studied us far less than other stepfamily members. That matters—but of far greater concern to me is that we aren't fully visible to ourselves. Most of us attend closely to the needs of others. We try to do well by the children and nurture our marriages. We strive to create warm homes and strengthen our new families. And then, seemingly out of the blue, something happens that makes us feel like outsiders, hanging on at the margins of the parent-child relationships that predated us.

Invisibility doesn't feel good. We want, rightly, to be seen, acknowledged, valued. And feeling invisible isn't good for us, either. If we think we're invisible, we can excuse ourselves from grappling honestly with our emotions and the damage we sometimes endure or impose. Even worse, feeling like we're invisible can prevent us from noticing and enjoying the love that may actually be flowing our way. And besides, we are not actually invisible. We are there, right in the middle of our wonderful, difficult, ever-changing families, visible to anyone who is willing to notice. Loving and being loved. Struggling and improvising. Yearning for a home that's life giving for all, including us, and sometimes finding just that.

This book brings stepmothers out of the shadows. But I've discovered that *writing* about stepmothering is almost as complicated as *being* a stepmother. Women who make commitments to love and care for a partner's child do so in many different personal, cultural, and economic contexts, producing countless specific patterns of parental work and relationship. I honor all such women, whatever their social location, identity, or marital status. While I earnestly hope that this book will be helpful to readers across a wide range of circumstances, however, it is unavoidably shaped by my own experience. I hope this book will encourage other stepmothers to share their own stories and insights.

Another complication is that my own story is entangled with stories that belong first of all to others, in this book as in life. When sharing family stories, I have worked very hard to speak only from and for my own experience and never to presume that I know what others were thinking at one point or another. If I have failed to meet this standard at certain points or have offended in any other way, I apologize.

A few years ago, I sent an email to my stepdaughter telling her I was writing an essay that included some scenes from her childhood. Did she have any objections? When I showed her a draft, she asked for just one revision. "Please use my name," she said. She wanted to be visible, just as she had struggled to feel visible in both of the households to which she belonged as a child. "Although I was a welcome member of both homes," she has written, "I was not a necessary part of either's design." While I didn't agree that she was unnecessary to either family, I honored her desire to be known by name. She has a beautiful and unusual name that belonged to her father's great-great-grandmother. Even so, I've decided not to use her real name in this book, and I've also changed the names of "Kristen's" husband and children. I'm not trying to cloak anyone's identity, which is easy enough to figure out these days. Instead, I'm trying to clarify—for myself, family members, and readers—that this story is mine. When most of us think about stepfamilies, our attention and concern rightly go first to the children. In this book, I'm working hard to spotlight a different corner, hoping that doing so will benefit not only stepmothers but also the other members of their families.

I sent a similar email to Kristen's mother, whom I also mentioned in that essay. She too was agreeable, except for one thing. Trying to achieve some verbal variety, I had referred to myself in one sentence as Kristen's "other mother." I am not her other mother, Bekka pointed out. Kristen only has one mother, and she is that mother. I am Kristen's stepmother. If I would make that change, she wrote, she could readily approve the rest of the essay. I didn't even need to ask for her permission if I wrote about our family in the future, she added; "I trust you." I made the change but continue to ask for her permission when I publish things that mention her, though I haven't asked her to check specific pages. This approach—share information but don't pry into or supervise the details—is similar, in a way, to how we've balanced our separate relationships with Kristen. In this book, I have changed the names of "Bekka" and her husband, Kristen's stepfather.

Mark—my husband, Kristen's father, Bekka's ex—was also supportive of that initial essay and now of this book. Recently I asked him if he thought our marriage would have lasted if Kristen and I had not gotten along. "Of course," he replied. I hope he's right, but after my research for this book, I'm also aware of how damaging to marriages stepfamily conflicts can be. Mark's answer was wonderful, and I'm grateful for it: what he was saying is that our marriage belongs first of all to the two of us, and he trusts that it's strong enough that it could have survived more stepfamily difficulty than we have encountered. I share that trust (and attribute it more to God's grace than to our own strength). Still, I'm relieved and delighted that Kristen and I do get along. That happened partly because Mark was such a loving father to her and such a supportive husband to me.

I thank all three for allowing me to share aspects of our family story, but the perspective here is mine alone. I write as a stepmother—in a voice that is too often silent, or silenced, in conversations about families today.

2
ORIGINS

Here's a short, familiar story: A couple with a child splits up. Two new families form, and the child, now a member of both families, travels back and forth between them. The story is so familiar that it may feel ordinary, easy, no big deal. But for me, the experiences the story relates are not at all humdrum and easy to digest.

I've lived this story—together with my (second) husband Mark, his (first) wife Bekka, and their (only) child Kristen. After a divorce of my own, I joined the story as Mark's spouse. That's how I became a stepmother. Follow the story a little further, and Bekka marries a man with two sons; she becomes a stepmother too.

My divorce and Mark's happened independently after each of our first marriages found its own pitiful path to disaster.

But even though these divorces were distinct—as other breakups also were and are—it's hard not to see both as belonging to a single massive cultural shift gaining momentum in the ten years after each of us said our initial marriage vows.

Ours was the generation born and raised during the years of high fertility that followed the Second World War. Trends that had taken hold earlier in the century—fewer and later marriages, a declining birth rate—reversed themselves, and married-with-children became the national ideal. As suburbs were built and consumer-oriented nuclear families seized the popular imagination, Dad-and-Mom-and-Dick-and-Jane households multiplied from coast to coast; from 1948 to 1958, 85 percent of all new housing built in the United States was in the suburbs.

Many Americans were excluded by race, economics, or sexual orientation from adopting the male breadwinner/female homemaker ideal—and some were simply not attracted to this way of life. Even so, such families, including the families Mark and I grew up in, were touted as normative in the media, at church, in public life, and in workplaces, where women were less present than they'd been during the war. After a brief postwar spike, the divorce rate plummeted.

A little later, ours was also the generation most heavily influenced by a set of powerful challenges to this American family ideal—challenges that heated up during the 1960s and boiled over during the 1970s. Astute observers within those decades suspected that postwar American marriages and families were not nearly as sturdy as 1950s popular media implied—but just about everyone would later agree that certain events during the next decade put further pressure on supposedly normative patterns. Between 1965 and 1980, the rate of divorce more than doubled. A social psychologist who studies marriage, Eli Finkel, attributes this rapid shift primarily to changes in culture that burrowed deep into individual souls: "self-expression" was hailed, and widely adopted, as an indispensable sign of the good life. Other historians notice scientific and economic changes that supported these same developments—the availability of birth control pills beginning in 1960, for example, and the increasing access of women to higher education and work beyond the home. Many women could now imagine and handle life apart from marriage, the institution on which most women in history had depended for both physical sustenance and social belonging. Those in oppressive situations could now leave. As divorce became both more common and more accepted, laws changed as well. In 1969, California became the first state to allow "no-fault" divorce proceedings, which simplified couples' ability to terminate marriages.

The divorce rate peaked during the early 1980s. If you plotted all the divorces of the last century on a graph, Mark's and mine would be riding the crest of a tidal wave. During these years, more marriages ended each year than began. This is when an immensely discouraging warning—"your chance of divorce is 50/50"—began to shape both public and personal conversations about marriage.

I was one of the casualties of this trend or, depending on how you look at it, one of the causes. I now can see that I participated in a major demographic shift. But believe me, at the time I did not feel like a statistic. When your heart has been ripped out, it's not much comfort to know that your experience is statistically normal. That said, I can't deny I was glad I did not stand out as uniquely unsuccessful in my personal life. I shudder to imagine the shame my aunt had to endure after her divorce in Texas in the 1930s. Today, divorce has lost its outward stigma in many communities, but individual feelings of failure and shame can still be hard to overcome. Those who end primary relationships not bound by marriage can also encounter such feelings.

These changes have led to the emergence of a new kind of stepfamily. Starting in the early 1970s, for the first time in history, more stepfamilies were formed after a divorce than after a death. In recent years, stepfamilies have become three times more likely to come into being after the bereavement of separation or divorce than after a partner's death. And not all of these new stepfamilies turn out to be permanent. The divorce rate is slightly higher in second marriages than in first.

When a social earthquake shakes the architecture of a given family form—for example, the Dad-and-Mom-and-Dick-and-Jane family—historians and anthropologists are not surprised. Across centuries and cultures, human beings have constructed countless forms of intimate bonding for mutual protection and care, arranging their lives and labor to provide for the needs of children, the aged, and those in between. To those living inside these arrangements, a given culture's pattern can seem natural, seamlessly joining how things are with assumptions about how things are meant to be. Such patterns can seem permanent. From the perspective of history, however, they are not. Family structures can and do change. One form weakens, people adapt, and another form emerges.

Today's stepfamilies can be seen as proof that one more shift within the ongoing historical process of family formation is taking place. The big picture is this: the high value placed on individual choice, in combination with a commitment to ongoing personal development, has merged with material factors—longer life spans, changing career patterns, lack of structural support for childrearing and family life—to make commitments less likely to last over the course of a lifetime. In this context, trying again after a marriage ends makes sense, with stepfamilies part of the evolution of family.

American marriage itself is becoming "deinstitutionalized," according to sociologist Andrew Cherlin, who cites studies showing that formerly shared norms defining people's behavior and roles are becoming more individual and flexible and less tied to traditional expectations. When Cherlin first identified this trend in a study of stepfamilies back in the late 1970s, he predicted a subsequent process of reinstitutionalization: over time, stepfamilies would develop a new, stabilizing set of norms and expectations about, say, relationships between stepparents and step-children. Instead, Cherlin later observed, deinstitutionalization extended its reach, becoming a force that shapes first-marriage families as well. What Cherlin didn't fully anticipate was how much elements of choice and flexibility would increase even in families where divorce and remarriage have not occurred.

In a sense, the stepfamilies that emerged due to increased divorce and remarriage were part of a larger trend toward diversity in family forms that has also opened space and visibility for queer families. Another sociologist, Megan

M. Sweeney, has drawn on Cherlin's categories to argue that stepfamilies are especially well suited to this moment in the ongoing history of how people form families of many kinds. Think of it this way: The emphasis on choice sways vast swatches of contemporary American culture—what we eat, what we wear, what we believe. Likewise, Americans want to choose the shape of their families. A second or third attempt, built over the remains of an earlier attempt, may provide hope of a fresh family that better accords with a person's hopes and values.

Studying stepfamilies, Sweeney argues, thus opens a revealing window onto how Americans more generally think about families and the significant issues they face. Fluidity and choice rule—for adults, anyway. "The incompletely institutionalized" character of stepfamilies means that they "offer individuals considerable latitude of choice when negotiating processes associated with family formation, maintenance, and functioning." One result is "unprecedented levels of voluntary partnership turnover."

Many kinds of stepfamilies exist today—proliferating alongside numerous variously shaped "nontraditional" families. It's impossible to describe an ideal based on a specific structure, and those who have an investment in calling one family or another "ideal" often fail to understand the bigger picture. For myself, I honor and hold respect for all mutually committed households as families, whether with one parent or two, of one gender or more, legally married or not, presently at peace or undergoing difficulties. Some families—even when they appear to fit a first-marriage, Mom-and-Dad-with-kids "ideal"—are broken by abuse or intense conflict. Other families whose members have endured many losses along the way become oases of nurture and hospitality.

Even with changes and ruptures, the persistent human desire to give ourselves to one another in ways that endure amazes me. I have yearned all my life for trustworthy and lasting relationships—and I know I'm not alone in this yearning. We all long to find for ourselves and to provide for our loved ones safe, reliable homes. Few couples marry and have children hoping that someday their own little girl will be shuttling back and forth between their own two separate households.

And these safe and reliable homes for which we yearn? They are part of how things are supposed to be. It's a profound human desire—though not one we fragile and fallible human beings can ever fully secure. Sometimes death visits a family, snatching a parent away. And sometimes, as for Mark and me, once treasured relationships are irretrievably broken. Most of us understand that ended relationships of either kind have created loss for everyone concerned, and especially for our children. This does not mean that the new families we are making are inferior or illegitimate. It means, rather, that we are learning to be honest about the losses in our past and more fierce and tender in our care for one another in the present.

It's complicated. Just plain complicated, obviously, but also complicated because the members of stepfamilies come to their roles with few clear guidelines about what is expected of them as stepparents, stepchildren, or step-siblings. Once people have created these unexpected second (or more) families, the lingering, sometimes haunting, question is, What obligations do they have to one another? Are family newcomers supposed to role-play Mom and Dad or keep their distance? How should they show respect for the parent/child relationships that predated the step-family? And what respect do these newcomers themselves deserve?

In our society, there are no set answers to such questions. When asked, people can usually say what they think they owe their own parents or children or siblings, the ones to whom they are related by blood or adoption. However, they typically find it much tougher to answer questions about how they see their obligations to steprelatives. In the abstract, these responses aren't surprising: people feel more obligation to their unhyphenated, usually genetic kin. When researchers asked 2,691 Americans how obligated they would feel to help family members in need, responses tipped strongly in that direction (for example, in the most lopsided case, 85 percent felt obligated to help their parents, but only 56 percent felt obligated to help their stepparents).

Unless adoption occurs, a relationship between a stepparent and a stepchild has no legal status or protection, regardless of whether a stepparent has married the child's parent. I often hear of the heartbreak suffered by stepparents whose relationship with their stepchild's parent has ended; after years of shared life and love, the stepparent's access to and relationship with the parent's children abruptly comes to an end. True, sometimes the opposite happens: I know a woman whose close relationship with her stepchildren has long outlived her divorce from their father. She is one of the proudest and happiest grandmothers I know. But this outcome is far from assured.

Julie Gosselin, a clinical psychologist in Canada, has written about the intrinsic vulnerability of the stepmother's role from a perspective that is both personal and professional. When she and "George" separated after living together, with his two young daughters, for seven years, Gosselin found that her "membership card" in the family had been revoked. She hoped to continue a relationship with the girls, but this would depend on them as well as on her (one relationship endured, one did not). After years of full-fledged family life, she was not only single again but also childless; she felt abandoned, confused, and alone, as if she had "shed this motherhood like a worn jacket." She experienced solidarity with other women who mother "at the margins: foster mothers, non-custodial mothers, mothers who have lost contact with their children, and mothers of children who have disappeared or passed away." Like them, she had become an "invisible mother whose pain [was] socially ignored."

Even when outcomes are happy, vulnerability is woven into the new, dear relationships into which stepparents enter—something that is rarely noted amid overwhelming, completely justifiable concern for the vulnerability of stepchildren. During the early stages of my relationship with Mark, before we decided to get married, I felt this vulnerability sharply. Was I giving my heart to Kristen, only to risk losing her as well as her father? Even after Mark and I married, this feeling returned from time to time across the years. The visitation agreement underlying Kristen's time with me was an agreement between Mark and Bekka. If he were to die, would I still be able to see her? Probably so, I hoped, but not as frequently, and likely in a less familiar and familial way. One study of adult stepchildren found that it is difficult for most to sustain familial relationships with their widowed stepparents, once the person who was the child's biological parent and the stepparent's spouse is no longer present. But this is not always the case, especially when long-term closeness, shared values, and inclusive communication during the deceased's dying and burial have nourished the bonds between them.

How deeply can the members of stepfamilies rely on one another? Ideally, we would never need to ask such a question, so busy would we be showering each other with love and care. But we do need to ask it, not only because of human failings common to all, but also because of the undefined character of stepfamily roles. The members of families untouched by divorce must also face questions about their obligations to one another, to be sure. But society communicates expectations that are far clearer in the biological or adoptive case than in the step case, whether the obligations finally get fulfilled or not.

Questions of obligation and mutual reliance almost never arrive in the abstract, however. Each stepmother has to work this out right in the middle of a life that is cluttered by other concerns and in a society where parenting of any kind is challenging. Meanwhile, her spouse and stepchildren are simultaneously trying to figure things out as well.

* * *

One potent claim appears repeatedly in the clinical literature on stepfamilies: *stepmothers occupy the most difficult role in stepfamilies and often have the most problems and pain in becoming integrated into the new family.* I've searched for a study that proves this point, but I have found no single, persuasive source. Rather, this startling assertion seems to have emerged, in pieces, from the findings of numerous studies on stepfamilies and then to have been stitched together into a single claim by psychologists, social workers, and therapists who see an important truth here. On first thought, the claim strikes me as over the top. On second thought, I can't resist sharing it here, nor can I keep it out of my mind whenever I feel discouraged.

Back in the day, I would never have spoken (or even allowed myself to entertain) this thought, perhaps because I was so deeply committed to focusing on the impact of our situation on Kristen. Or maybe I simply escaped its force by becoming a stepmother under relatively favorable conditions. Research suggests that children between the ages of ten and sixteen are most likely to resist their new stepmothers, and Kristen was much younger when I came along. Tensions associated with "complex" stepfamilies—those to which both partners bring children—were absent. Kristen was the only child, originally, in our new stepfamily, so we did not have to negotiate conflicts among new stepsiblings. She, Mark, and I had time to adjust to one another without that complication. Further, Mark was fully engaged in Kristen's care, and Bekka did not try to subvert my relationship with Kristen. I had a much easier situation within which to learn my new role than many stepmothers do.

That said, stepchildren typically resent their stepmothers much more intensely than they do their stepfathers, researchers with the Virginia Longitudinal Study of Divorce and Remarriage discovered. The basic problem, this study suggests, lies in the expectations of domesticity and child-wrangling placed upon women by society—and by their own husbands. Stepmothers rarely have the option of stepping back from childcare; instead, "they find themselves in the center of the fray, [where] they are often expected to be nurturers to already difficult and suspicious children." Trying to meet their husbands' expectations, stepmothers try to create household order, often with wonderful intentions fueled by a genuine desire for family harmony. But when children harbor anger and resentment—as many do, and who can blame them?—this pattern can be dangerous.

"In our most contentious stepfamilies," these researchers reported, "a real demonizing of the stepmother often occurred. We heard stepmothers described by some stepchildren as 'evil,' 'malevolent,' 'wicked,' or as 'monsters,' and nicknamed 'Dog Face' or 'the Dragon.'" And human nature being what it is, the feeling can quickly become mutual. Rage at recalcitrant children who will not eat what's served, follow household rules, or carry on civil conversations erupts all over social media, Facebook pages, and websites where stepmothers gather.

The lead researcher in the Virginia study, E. Mavis Hetherington, attributes the gendered expectations that give rise to such conflicts primarily to the husbands of stepmothers. Fair enough, in many cases. When I search my own heart, however, I also discover these expectations deeply embedded there: my desires to nurture children, craft a home, and prepare meals for others are my own, even though I can see that they have been formed across the decades by life in a particular society and, especially, in my own family of origin. These are by no means the only desires I have: I also want, and have enjoyed, good work outside the home. But when I made chicken and dumplings for Kristen and Mark every Wednesday during the early months of our relationship, I was meeting expectations that came from within as well as from outside.

Whenever adults form new families, they bring with them prior family experiences that have shaped them personally and taught them what a family should and should not be—including experiences in the families they inhabited as children. That conditioning includes training, both explicit and implicit, in gender roles. Understandings of gender are changing, and, with effort, unhelpful lessons from the past can be unlearned. But even as men invest intentionally in nurture and domestic activities more than when I was a child, or when Kristen was, certain longstanding presumptions persist. Many people simply expect women to be good with children and to know how to create the material conditions of domestic peace. Not all women embrace these tasks, however, and the expectations embedded within these tasks can be maddening even for those who are willing to give them a try.

The 1998 movie *Stepmom* features a vivid portrayal of the gendered dance that often takes shape in stepfamilies. After two suburban parents—played by Susan Sarandon and Ed Harris—separate, their busy lives become even more hectic than before. New divisions of labor—who will drive the kids to school, who will root from the sidelines at their sporting events, who will do the laundry—make a hash of their demanding professional schedules. The dad's new girlfriend is game to help—and as the opening credits roll, she is making breakfast for two sullen middle schoolers. Cereal, homework, making plans for after-school activities: all the surface markers of parental intimacy are in place. But the kids are doing everything they can to make it clear that she's got it all wrong. Soon Sarandon whisks in to set things right: a better breakfast, a remembered medication, an in-joke with the kids. New divisions of labor will not be allowed to create new divisions of affection! (It probably doesn't help that the new girlfriend is played by Julia Roberts.)

Harris's character—a successful attorney who is a shockingly absent father—needs a partner to care for his children if he is to have them in his home at all. Thoughtlessly, he assumes that his fiancée will gladly and capably lift this load. She seems to make the same assumption, even though she is a successful professional photographer. Before his divorce, I suspect, this fictional father expected the same domestic heavy lifting from his wife, the children's mother. Watching this film, I see one incompetent parent, the father; one very good parent, the mother; and one stepmother, who is only okay at first but who is rapidly getting better.

Very good stepmothers are not altogether invisible in media and popular culture. The kind woman who raised Abraham Lincoln has long been celebrated for her capable fulfillment of this role, and many today admire Dr. Jill Biden as the stepmother of two boys, the sons of a widowed young senator from Delaware. On television, Florence Henderson as Carol Brady made stepmothering her bunch look easy. And when it comes to movies, it's not so hard to think of mainstream films besides *Stepmom* that include stepfamilies. As film critic Hampus Hagman notes, however, celluloid narratives rarely allow stepmothers to live with children whose mothers are still alive. When a father finds a second wife, Hollywood's writers typically choose or craft a story in which the first wife is dead, and if she's not they kill her off. (Think of *The Sound of Music*. Where is Frau von Trapp?) An admirable stepmother doesn't join the family primarily as a new wife, Hagman finds; instead, she is there as a "new mother." Ideally, she will turn out to be really great with the kids (think of Frau's successor, Maria). The "new mother" may even be selected by the kids (as she is in *Sleepless in Seattle*, in which a young boy risks his life in pursuit of a complete stranger who sounds on the radio as if she'd be a nice mother for him and a good wife for his dad). Even better, a stepmother can be anointed by a dying mother as her worthy replacement (keep reading for this scenario). In the preferred plot, a family briefly loses its ideal shape and has trouble finding a means of repair. (That's the drama.) But in the end, the family is "renuclearized"—one dad, one mom, kids. Meanwhile, the new woman—the stepmother—has enriched the plot with a touch of sexual frisson. Hagman's point? The nuclear family model is upheld and reinforced, even when a nuclear family has faltered. No vision emerges of stepfamilies of the more common kind—where more than two adults hold parental roles.

The uncomfortable presence of three adult caregivers might have been a problem for the Ed Harris, Susan Sarandon, and Julia Roberts characters in *Stepmom*—if the screenwriters had not written the problem out of the script. Sadly, to reach this resolution, they had to eliminate the mother. She develops terminal cancer, clearing the field for Roberts's character, Isabel, to become a stepmother all of them can be glad is present. In affirmation, Isabel's title is softened to the informal "stepmom." As the mother's health deteriorates, Isabel improvises her way into decent, then good, relationships with the children. She gets better at the everyday work of it—the breakfasts and the clothes. She also makes big mistakes—like losing young Ben in Central Park. Finding him provides one kind of resolution. Sarandon's admission that she once lost him too resolves even more. What is required of Isabel, finally, is to be clear about who is who. "You're not my mom," Ben tells Isabel in angry resistance to some simple request. "Thank God for that," she replies. Long beat—then an addition that shows both strategic aptitude and honest affection: "What I meant is, you already have a great mom; I just want some respect when you are here."

Stepmothering is not a role I ever imagined for myself until I met a particular man who already had a child. As months and years unfolded, our little trio tried to figure out who we were supposed to be to one another. The people who study stepfamilies have names for the roles we now occupied. Mark, Kristen, and I formed a "nonresidential" stepfamily. This stepfamily was "simple" because I did not bring any children to it.

Kristen was almost three when Mark and I started dating. Everyone concerned lived in the same urban neighborhood—I in my own apartment, Kristen with Bekka in a condo purchased with Mark shortly before Kristen's birth, Mark in a studio apartment nearby. He drove Kristen's preschool carpool a couple of days a week, spent one weeknight afternoon and evening with her, and had her overnight at his place almost every weekend.

Carefully, slowly, Mark decided it was time for me to meet his daughter. We made a plan, hoping to make this momentous-feeling encounter seem casual to her, and to us: I would stop by their favorite playground on one of the afternoons she spent with him. He was crazy about her, and proud, and eager for me to see, at last, the liveliness, the beauty, the spunk that captivated him so. But when I arrived at the playground, she lay down on the grass, curled up in a ball, and started whining. He took her back to his apartment, where he discovered that she had a fever. We comforted ourselves that things would go better when she felt well, and they did. A week later, the three of us spent a lovely hour in that same park. I took photos of Kristen and Mark frolicking on a green lawn on a sunny day, the sky a deep blue, her overalls a vibrant red, her braids as yellow as corn. We still treasure these pictures of the two of them, taken by an invisible third party.

On Wednesday evenings that fall and winter, I got to know Kristen better when she accompanied Mark to supper at my apartment. We ate chicken and dumplings every single week, initiating my if-it's-not-broken-don't-fix-it approach to childcare. Cleaning up after supper was the best part: I perched Kristen on a stool so that we could work side by side, washing each dish until our skin shriveled and then running into the living room to scare Mark with our witchy fingers. Before supper, and often after as well, Mark and I read aloud the stories Kristen had created at preschool—her teacher wrote them out on ruled manila paper—and admired the illustrations Kristen had drawn on the top half of each page.

I loved these evenings. But when tears came, Mark took over. He was the parent.

What was I? I wondered. A Mary Poppins figure? Daddy's fun friend?

We made a pretty terrific threesome for those few hours each week. At the same time, my role was tentative. I was always aware that Kristen's mother was part of the mix. Kristen talked of her and looked like her; there was no denying the primary hold each of them had on the other. I was treading on territory that was already occupied, and I knew it. I moved cautiously, slowly, sensing the damage a wrong word or action might cause. Mark had a rule he lived by with ease: one parent should never criticize the other in the presence of the child. As a prospective stepmother, I had to add another layer: not to criticize, obviously, but also not to co-opt. The stakes were high. I learned to behave.

Even so, that Bekka was there, and that I knew she was there, was not all bad. Looking back, the moment I understood this still surprises me. During Kristen's first sudsy visit to my apartment, I instantly sensed that this little girl knew how to have fun with an adult woman because she spent much of her time with a good one. I appreciated Bekka—and over time, she subtly communicated that she appreciated Mark's and my time with Kristen too. Bekka may have been glad to be relieved of intense single-parenting duties for a while, but it also seemed clear from the beginning that she wanted her daughter to have a strong relationship with her father. Mark and Bekka had to work out some painful things and had some tense moments, of course, and I realize as I write this that Bekka must have been upset by my involvement at certain points. But if she was, I was shielded by both Mark and Bekka from knowing it. More important, so was Kristen. Everyone concerned had the power to make the new arrangement workable or miserable. I thought then, and I still believe, that Bekka had the most power, because she could have turned Kristen against me if she had chosen to. That she did not use that power to harm our relationship, as far as I could ever tell, was an amazing grace.

It would be two years before Mark and I got married and I became a stepmother officially. But during those years, playing house with this delightful little girl and the man I was in love with intensified my own maternal longings and established domestic patterns that would persist in years to come. Mark was devoted to his daughter and would have been faithful in visitation and fatherhood with or without me. I was and am clear about that. In my own mind, however, I won a place in his life partly by supporting and enabling his parenting. Helping him to secure his parenthood was more important to me than establishing my own. As appropriate as this was when we were just dating, this priority persisted for decades, possibly at a cost to my own relationship with Kristen.

What are the obligations of a stepmother? For me, in part, a stepmother is to be a bridge, an enabler, a cohesive force between others whose relationship would endure even if she were not there, but which might grow stronger because she is.

Amid the fluidity of family life in the twenty-first century, to be a force of cohesion is no small thing. It's just possible that when future historians look back on twenty-first-century families, they will conclude that stepmothers were located at a nexus point in the landscape of change on which today's families live. This nexus stands at the crossroads of sorrow and hope; it is a place where past loss and future possibility converge. Living at a busy intersection is never easy—and this particular intersection is an emotionally dangerous one. Our role is not well-defined, and opportunities to hurt and be hurt are everywhere. But at this intersection, we may also find, if we look, avenues for love.

I don't want to wait for future historians to notice that stepmothers live at a crucial location on the landscape of change. I want my family and neighbors, and yours, to see us now. I want them to acknowledge that each stepmother's struggle to figure out what being a stepmother means, in her specific situation, is worth noticing and supporting. And I want stepmothers to see themselves. Ourselves. It's complicated, but trying to live wisely and well as stepmothers matters deeply, to others and to ourselves.

3

HOME

Anyone could walk directly from the Midway Airport parking lot to the gate in those days. So that's where I was, my eyes fixed on a slow-moving stream of arriving passengers, my heart in my throat as I wondered how Kristen would greet me. She and her mother had recently moved to Minneapolis, and Mark and I had moved to a college town in Indiana. Kristen's transitions between our households now propelled her across more distance and required of her more courage than when we all lived in Chicago. This was the first time I was picking her up, something her father usually did.

Finally she emerged, the last passenger down the Jetway. One of her hands was in the manicured grasp of a tall, pretty flight attendant, while the other clutched a stuffed bear named Newspaper, whose fur she had worn away with years of caresses. Kristen's narrow face was without expression, but her eyes swept urgently across the crowded gate area. When she saw me, relief flooded her features, and then came a little smile. I wanted to think her look conveyed something like joy, and maybe it did. I know I felt joy—that she had arrived, that she was safe, and that Mark and I would have a few days with her.

No touching was allowed until after I showed my ID and signed the airline's form. Then we erupted in chatter and hugs. I'm so happy to see you! How was your flight? What's happening in kindergarten? Want to go to the Dunes this weekend? Holding hands, we walked to the baggage claim and then to the car, where I put her suitcase in the trunk and strapped her into her seat.

Soon we were headed for home, an hour away, where Mark had just begun a new job. But was this my home? Sort of. A newlywed and a newcomer, I was still discovering the layout of the town and the shape of the marriage that had taken me there. And was this Kristen's home? No, it was not. We had all agreed that her home, her one home, was to be with her mother. When Mark and Bekka divorced, their therapist advised them to make sure that everyone agreed about where Kristen's home was; give her that foundation, he urged. And they did. Kristen lived with her mother. She visited her father. Home was in Minneapolis. Valparaiso,

Indiana, was where she went for visits one weekend each month, every other Christmas, and substantial portions of other holidays and school vacations.

As I drove, I wondered how all these places fit together—for Kristen, for Mark, and for me. How should I think of the house where Mark was waiting to greet us?

Home. One of our deepest hungers is to know where it is and to trust that our place there is assured. Often home has a specific address—it is a dwelling, on a street, in a neighborhood, with a climate and a cuisine. It's the island Odysseus struggles to return to after twenty years of war and wandering. It's the mount where exiles once learned the songs they cannot sing beside the rivers of Babylon. It's the ancestral village refugees are forced to flee at the beginning of their dangerous journeys across sea lanes and international borders. But sometimes home's location is uncertain, and its features are shrouded in mist. Where, and what, is home? We yearn for it, but often it's beyond our reach and even beyond our conceiving.

The children of divorced parents are especially likely to wonder what home is, and where, researcher Elizabeth Marquardt discovered when she asked hundreds of adult children of divorce to reflect on their experience. Navigating "between two worlds," many of them reported, was one of the weightiest challenges they faced while growing up. Indeed, "between two worlds" is the title of Marquardt's thoughtful book, which passionately urges adults to take seriously the impact of divorce on the inner lives of children, including those who appear to have come through their parents' breakup just fine. The alternating currents of a child's attachment to each parent can create a painful force field. When you are living with one, you miss the other. When your hair color and last name match those of one household, you appear to be a misfit in the other. When new spouses and siblings take up space in one or another parent's home and heart, you feel like an outsider in the very places where your insider status should be most secure.

The emotional wallop of the two-worlds problem often comes into focus during moments of physical transition between households. Marquardt, herself a child of divorce, remembers her own "frequent sad departures," and she has also heard from others about the hardship of traveling between their parents' homes. The kids learn to do what's expected, she says, but the pain is real. "As little children we were able to walk down an airplane jetway by ourselves," she writes, "leaving our mother or father behind, with a matter-of-fact coolness that few children from intact families could approximate or imagine." With each departure, the scab would again be picked off the wound of loss. The impending arrival might provide some salve, to be sure, even some gladness, because it would bring a reunion with the parent previously left behind. But still. Transitions are hard. And often the difficulty is compounded because the adults don't want to admit just how hard all the moving back and forth really is. Marquardt says that she and other children tried to hide their pain to spare the feelings of the adults involved. She may not have realized it, but her parents and stepparents were probably trying to hide their pain to spare her feelings too. At least that is what happened for Mark and me. Recalling this, I don't mean to imply that the adults' pain overrides the child's. I just mean to notice it and to empathize with those adults who experience it.

Caring now for grandchildren who are the age Kristen was then but who haven't had to go through the back-and-forth she endured, I find it astounding that our little girl—pig-tailed and clutching a toy as she headed down the Jetway—was able to do so without a meltdown. I also find it astounding that we adults allowed it and even more astounding that we ourselves could bear it. The images that linger are of the small traveler, the one with the yellow braids and the threadbare stuffed animal. But there was also a teenager, lugging a backpack of homework between the upper and lower Midwest. How many high schoolers would willingly embrace a back-and-forth schedule like this?

Occasionally a divorce creates a distance that cannot be traversed by jet or any other means of transport. I have a young teenaged friend who never sees her father. He used to show up a few times a year, but his insult-laden visits proved so upsetting that she cut them off, with the full support of her mother and, it turned out, with little objection from him. There is no doubt which of two parental worlds she inhabits. This young woman may eventually need to do some psychological navigating between the legacies of these two worlds, but for now she is choosing not to do so.

In another family I know, two boys moved back and forth between houses just a few blocks apart. You might think this way of arranging joint custody would run smoothly—the boys had the same school, friends, and teams in both places, and even a misplaced piece of homework could be readily retrieved. To these boys, however, the distinct worlds occupied by their mother and their father seemed light-years apart. There were times when one or the other simply refused to change houses on the appointed day. "I'm staying here," they'd say—and this happened, over time, not just at one house but also at the other. In other cases, the kids stay put while the parents move in and out. This may preserve a certain sense of home as place, though with the likelihood that some sense of dislocation still remains. Is home a specific place or a certain set of people?

As far as I can discover, no excellent study has concluded that a certain living arrangement is superior to others. A shuttling child? Rotating parents? Limiting visitations to certain seasons? My gut says that living in the same area must be better than being separated by an airplane ride; I admire a divorced friend who turned down an excellent job in order to stay close to his sons. At the same time, I don't find the prospect of too much proximity appealing—putting a little distance between former spouses makes emotional sense in many cases. For most of us, options are limited by finances and sometimes by the unfitness of one of the parents. Most of the time, everyone is just trying to do the best they can under the circumstances.

Just after finishing kindergarten, I too walked down a Jetway without my parents. Not because of divorce—my parents would have a good, long marriage—but as a treat, or so they said. Grandmother and Granddaddy Bass accompanied me. They and my maternal grandparents lived far from us but near each other, and the four of them wanted to spend the summer pampering their eldest grandchild. Years later, when I asked my mother how this trip could have seemed like a good idea, she said that I had been so mature for my age—though by then I had guessed the truth, which was that she had had her hands full with a two-year-old, a newborn, and a move to a new house near yet another Navy base, her sixth move since my birth. Pictures of me taken that summer show a little girl whose dresses are adorable and whose face is blank. Unable to get my thick blonde hair under control, Grandmother had it cut short and permed so that it would be stylish in the portrait she had made. I look six going on forty. After a few weeks, my other grandparents escorted me back to California by train. Sitting with my mother's mother in the observation car at dusk, I saw a bird of prey flying above the desert, a long snake dangling from its beak. That is the clearest memory I have from that summer. I don't remember meeting my baby brother or being fussed over in Texas. I remember a desolate view from the train.

As a stepmother, I found airports, flights, and distances crossed upsetting. Kristen, on the other hand, seems to have taken the travel involved in our arrangement in stride. Years after she had outgrown her status as an unaccompanied minor, she reflected back on her childhood trips between Minneapolis and Valparaiso. "Oddly, I felt content during those flights, equally divided between my two lives, counting the flashes of light at the end of the wingtip," she wrote. What threw her off, far more, was having to alternate between "two lives"—lives that featured different foods, different landscapes, different rituals, different styles, and different approaches to housework and shopping. Mark and Bekka shared enough values that each trusted the other to provide a safe and nurturing space for their daughter, and Kristen (outwardly, at least) went along with the prevailing division of time in each place, adapting to the ethos of whichever household she occupied at the moment. That said, Kristen has also reported that a host of small differences between the two households sometimes left her conflicted about the right shape of everyday life. Home is made of small, material moves like these—what to eat, what to wear, and how to pray (or not).

Looking back on my own childhood in a Navy family that moved frequently, I don't remember lacking a sense of home. Home was where my parents and siblings were. Home was the place where my father mowed the lawn and my mother cooked fried chicken, rice, peas, and gravy each Sunday after church. Home harbored our piano, our books, and our familiar cups and plates. Maybe I would have a stronger, or at least a different, sense of home if my entire childhood had been spent in a single house, on a single landscape. But even as we moved, I knew where I belonged. Home was about the people, not the location.

If home is about the people we share it with, the kids who move back and forth between two worlds are not the only ones who must adjust. The parents and stepparents who receive these kids also experience change when the kids show up. Depending on the day or season, as defined by visitation schedules over which they by now have little control, noise levels and dirty dishes suddenly multiply. There are different faces across the table and different shows on the television. The shape and pace of familiar everyday activities shift. Somehow, the adults are supposed to hold things together; that is, they're supposed to keep the meals, bedtimes, work, and fun flowing for this new mix of people, people (including themselves) who are accustomed to doing things differently most of the time. To top it all off, they're supposed to keep everything flowing with as much equanimity and cheer as possible, even if their visitors show almost none. For the specific adult in each household who takes the lead in matters of food and cleanliness, the adjustment can be massive. At stake are both her care of children and her own sense of home.

The phrase *Funny Sauce*—the title of a quirky memoir by screenwriter Delia Ephron—says it all. "I don't like chicken in funny sauce," Ephron's eight-year-old stepdaughter fussed, rejecting yet another of the dishes her stepmother had struggled to please her with. In a series of vignettes that follows Ephron's relationship with her two stepchildren into their teenage years, she recounts the insults and resistance she encountered as the family's least-loved member—the "green lollipop" neither child wanted to get stuck with. After years of trying to care for these kids, Ephron began to feel used. She knew that the rest of the world saw her as a wicked stepmother; but she finally figured out that she was actually Cinderella, the oppressed servant, "cooking and driving the coach-and-four." She had thought the castle was hers, but it turned out that she was just the scullery maid. Need to impose discipline on the inhabitants? Don't even think about it.

I remember a green lollipop moment of my own, a moment when something Kristen said crystallized what was bothering me. Unfortunately, I don't have an amusing two-word phrase to sum it up.

As I came in from the yard one summer day, I overheard Mark and Kristen talking in the family room. She was six years old, and she was crying.

"I want to be with my own mommy in my own kitchen," she said.

I retreated, letting Mark continue to cuddle and console her. Then, alone on the porch, I cried too. I understood Kristen's homesickness, and I did not begrudge her desire. But hearing her express it so directly made me wonder anew where I fit, in her life and even in our kitchen, the domestic space she and I so often shared. Was I just the scullery maid?

I couldn't imagine where I might appear within Kristen's picture of home, and my own image of home was blurry as well. But I did know what I desired. I wanted to be with my own child in my own kitchen.

It took me a long time to sort out my sense of what and where home was—Kristen's, but also my own. In my first years as a stepmother, it hurt me to say the word *home*, since the word pointed away from the dwelling Kristen shared with her father and me for a significant portion of each year, a dwelling that included a room for her, a Strawberry Shortcake bike in the garage, and a really fun playmate next door. And so I avoided the word altogether. "Time to go back to Minneapolis," I'd say as we packed for her flight. If we were at the playground in Valparaiso and it was time to start preparing dinner, it would be "Shall we go back to our house?" rather than "Time for us to head home." I was working hard to create a nurturing space for her and Mark, and it felt pretty cozy when the three of us were there together. But I had to mind my tongue.

I understood then, and I still understand, that having a clear sense of one stable grounding place was important for this child's development, and I have encouraged families in similar circumstances to take the therapist's advice on this point. At the same time, this formulation overlooks something important. It would not do to define her father's house as a not-home, an antihome, a place where you'd better be careful not to feel as if you really belong. Keep the lines clear! Don't let your guard down! Such cautions would not be good for anyone. Whenever Kristen was with us, our house needed to be a place where she would find what any child needs each day. Rest. Nourishment. Play. Love. If she were to thrive—indeed, if all of us were to thrive and sustain the relationships we desired and deserved—this Indiana house of ours needed to be a home as well. For her, for us. Not her main home, not her one true home, but a home even so. A home that holds her in an embrace that is secure—while at the same time being poised to open its arms wide.

This can be more difficult than it might seem. How do you craft a space that welcomes even as it frees, a dwelling that receives an additional resident with an open heart and then lets her go, again and again? One part of the answer is to avoid clutching such a resident too tightly, much as you might wish to do so. Mark and I needed to learn not only to hold Kristen close during our limited time with her but also to let our home become one more launching pad for the flights she had it within her to make.

* * *

A few months before Mark and I moved to Valparaiso, my parents traveled to Chicago for our wedding. My mother, an elementary school librarian, brought along a gift for Kristen: a beautifully illustrated edition of *The Wizard of Oz*. This long chapter book is pretty complicated for a child barely four-and-a-half years old; in later years, I've never been able to get children younger than six or seven to sit still for it. But when Kristen got fussy during the simple reception being held in my apartment, my mother hustled her off to the back bedroom. They did not emerge until several chapters later, by which time Dorothy was already traveling the Yellow Brick Road. Kristen has an amazing gift for taking in stories, to be sure, and my mother had a wondrous way of reading them. But I had a feeling that this story also tapped into something distinctive: Kristen's connection to a heroine who flies involuntarily from her home to a place of new friendships. For a little while that summer, I actually had Kristen convinced that the girl in the story was my own younger self—or, more truly, she had me convinced that she accepted this grandiose claim of mine, pretending not to see the wink that typically accompanied my claim. The story of Dorothy Gale's dislocation and homecoming was one that resonated with us both.

The Wizard of Oz is just one of the many classics of children's literature that feature displaced heroines or heroes. Such beloved books endure, in part, because they tap deep into the psychology of childhood, where the need for security wrestles with the desire for adventure, the fear of isolation with the appeal of discovery—and, in a different way, into the psychology of adults as well. Often such literary protagonists are displaced against their will. They get lost in one way or another early in the story, but they find their way home by the end. The surprise, the learning, is that home turns out to be different on the last page than it was on the first, as Dorothy discovers upon returning to Kansas. Home has changed, and so has she.

In *The Secret Garden*, by Frances Hodgson Burnett, a favorite book of ours during the summer Kristen was six, the heroine never returns to the place she was living at the beginning. After the sudden death of her parents, agents of the British Empire in India, Mary Lennox is forced to move to the north of England, where an uncle will take her in. His gloomy estate on the moors holds loneliness and terror rather than welcome and warmth. Mary's journey home will not take her back to her birthplace; instead, it will be accomplished through transformations that happen right on that isolated estate, as she discovers and cultivates the gifts hidden there. She ventures into the cold, dark corridors of the antiquated mansion and finds a friend; she unravels and gains empathy for the suffering of those who seem uncaring and distant; she discovers kinship with the natural world. She gains confidence in herself and connections to others. Home finally emerges through her own effort—the hard work of clearing, planting, and sharing a once neglected garden that will become a place of healing and community.

While I don't mean to equate Kristen's visits to her dad and me with Dorothy's trip to Oz or Mary's voyage from India to Yorkshire, Kristen's visits *did* take some heroism on her part. As she grew—from five, to ten, and through her teens—she needed more than a father and a stepmother to provide a world worth visiting. Ultimately, her own courageous forays into the territory surrounding our family's house were what would make our potentially boring town a place where she could willingly spend some of her time. And once she found a place to make these forays, her courage was astounding. For her, that place was the stage.

Kids need more than a house furnished with caring adults and plenty of good books and toys. They also need a larger community in which to grow; they need somewhere to risk themselves as they discover the world and where they belong in it. The Young Actors Shakespeare Workshop was that somewhere for Kristen during the summers she spent with us. For four weeks each year, she was one of twenty children, ages 8 to 16, who performed a Shakespeare play on our local college campus. The director might shorten the play a little, but the words were all Shakespeare's. No censoring the dirty bits. No simplifying the difficult language. Some of the youngsters had parts with just a few lines, while others had to learn hundreds. They worked to figure out the emotions being expressed in their lines, and they learned to move about on the stage. They became actors, and they became friends.

It was astonishing to see Kristen on stage for the first time, strutting onto the outdoor set, tiny but holding herself tall in an adorable black-and-white jester's costume tailored just for her, as Touchstone, in *As You Like It.* And it was still astonishing, years later, when she poured all the drama of her young life into "Out, damned spot!" Mark and I were her biggest fans; for these few weeks each year, we got to be the soccer parents, the band parents, the stage parents— all those kinds of parents we did not get to be most of the time. And others in our town came to appreciate Kristen too—our friend John Steven Paul, who directed the workshop; the parents of the other actors, who made up most of the audience; and some friends her own age.

Mark and I could not make a good enough home-away-from-home on our own. It took a village. And it took Kristen's cooperation. Her effort. Her courage.

* * *

In the meantime, I found my own way home. Maybe I would have recognized more readily that I was home if we had lived in a region of the country I knew better, or in one of the great cities I find so appealing. But that wasn't where we were. Homecoming had to happen, for me, in a county seat town in Indiana. This was not my first choice, but it was (and still is) a choice I made, in a place I have come to embrace.

I knew I was home when I found myself welcoming others to this place where I had once been a stranger. Looking back, I recall what it felt like to settle in at last, after years of longing. Oddly, the settling in was also an opening up. I remembered an image from the Hebrew Bible's prophet Isaiah, who preached to a band of refugees as their wandering also came to an end, in a homeland for which they had long been yearning. "Enlarge the site of your tent," he urged them as they arrived. Now that they were home, they could set up their tents in confidence and joy—but they also needed to stretch out the tents' fabric sides to make room for others. Being at home, their families would grow. Being at home, they could invite others into the shade.

I was home at last when I realized I felt secure enough to roll up the tent flaps of my Indiana house to invite others in. Kristen was the first among these, but over time, others came too. Surprisingly, one who showed up was

Bekka, who stayed with us one night each summer when she came down to see Kristen perform in that year's play. For that one night each year, she moved into the bottom bunk in Kristen's room, before going to campus the next day to become, in Kristen's eyes, the honored member of the audience.

So there Bekka was, and there Kristen was, and there Mark and I were. And I could see, at last, that the place we all four shared, for that single night, was indeed my own true home, the fruit of the marriage Mark and I had made together over the years. It was now a place of welcome, built by partners now strong enough to remember the past while simultaneously being free from the pains of the past. Perhaps this sense of rest—this confidence that I had indeed found my home after a long and messy journey—explains why a line from Saint Augustine had become so dear to me: "What shall I render to you, oh God, that now my memory can recall all these things, but my heart is not afraid of them?"

Bekka's visits were a little awkward for me at first, but after a couple of years, I managed them easily. Indeed, I realized, I was glad to have her in the home Mark and I so often shared with Kristen—this home that was not Kristen's primary home but that was not her antihome either.

4

FERTILITY

If there was ever a day in my life when I did not want to have children, I have forgotten that day. I wasn't a little girl who played with dolls, and I never dreamed of becoming a kindergarten teacher. I just couldn't imagine for myself a good life that did not include being the one to whom a child turned for help, the one who was the preferred reader of bedtime stories and baker of cookies, the one whose lap was the most desired spot in the house. I suppose I wanted to be a mother because my own mother mothered me well, while also drawing me, the oldest of her four, into the work of caring for the younger children. Long after my siblings and I had grown up and dispersed, I often felt that big sister was my best role.

So how could it be that I was thirty-two and childless?

*   *   *

"Next month," he would say. Not Mark, but the husband of my twenties, the husband I had before I got divorced and moved to Chicago. Sure, we'll have a baby, but not yet. Let's wait a little while longer. We'll start trying next month. We spent three disheartening years like that, always on the verge of jumping into parenthood, or so I thought, but we never took the leap. My desire to become pregnant was so strong that I barely noticed how weak my husband's desire was for me—about as weak, I can now admit, as mine was for him. Thank God I didn't take the advice of some foolish friends to trick him into conception by poking holes in my diaphragm.

I was thirty when I told my parents that my marriage was over. I wept noisily into the phone.

"I am so sorry to disappoint you," I sobbed.

"You have never disappointed us," my mother replied in her warm, familiar voice. "We love you. Let us know how we can help."

"But I thought you wanted grandchildren," I stammered through my tears.

"If we want more children, we'll have them ourselves," said my father. It was too late for that, of course; he just wanted me to know that I did not need to propagate for my parents' sake. Rarely had a sentence communicated such grace to me. A huge burden fell from my shoulders, my heart, my belly. This did not, however, eliminate my longing to bear and raise a child.

When I look back on that thirty-two-year-old woman who was so desperate to have a child, I can now see how very fortunate she was, in spite of her grief and longing—fortunate, at least, when compared to countless other women across cultures and centuries. For most women in the history of the world, personal and social survival has been closely linked to the bearing of children. For those women, bearing children was and is necessary to gain a place at a table with food on it, a place in a cabin or cave, a place where people know your name and care for you when you are ill. My situation was different and in most ways stronger. Childlessness did not put my physical sustenance and standing in society at risk. I had a good education and a good job. I lived in an urban neighborhood and belonged to a community where some people lived in traditional families while others were developing less traditional forms of love and belonging. At parties, I joined a sizable circle of divorced friends in belting out Gloria Gaynor's rollicking disco break-up anthem, "I Will Survive." I knew I would survive, even at the time. It's just that I really, really wanted to be a mother.

During the early years of my relationship with Mark, I poured myself into Kristen's care, aware that this might be the one chance at parenting I was going to get. I loved Mark, I loved Kristen, and I loved the little household we created together. But I wanted more, and eventually, so did Mark. The experiences we shared with Kristen confirmed our sense that we could be good parents together. They also heightened my desire to have a child with Mark—and, fortunately, his desire to have a child with me.

That's the pretty way of putting it—and this pretty way of putting it is true, as far as I'm able to know the truth in a mysterious matter like this. But there is also another way of looking at how my stepmothering in those years was related to my insistent desire to bear children of my own. This alternative way of explaining what was happening during those years is less pretty, but I suspect it contains a grain of truth. This explanation is based on the idea that deeper forces than we consciously understand drive our behavior, especially our sexual behavior. If you believe, as I do, that we humans are often propelled by motives of which we are not aware and passions we hide even from ourselves, this explanation is worth considering.

Thinkers influenced by the work of Charles Darwin, the nineteenth-century scientist who developed the theory of evolution, contend that the behavior of animals, including humans, is ultimately motivated by the drive to spread their own genes into the next generation. These thinkers don't claim that such motivation is conscious or that the bestowal of genes is deliberate; rather, inherited instincts buried deep in the subconscious shape this behavior. As a result, humans and other animals tend to mate and offer nurture in ways that advance their individual reproductive success. These tendencies emerge thoughtlessly in our responses to others. We are not thinking about advancing our own genes while we're having sex, but most of us are pleased when we have children who look like us.

This theory makes some sense—but it also gives rise to some tough questions. For example, Why do some adults expend great energy caring for offspring to whom they are not genetically related? And why, in particular, would step-mothers do this? A Darwinian answer has emerged from research on peregrine falcons and certain other bird species. According to scientists Martin Daly and Margo Wilson, this research shows that "step-parental investment is often the price paid for future breeding opportunities with the genetic parent." In other words, when a mother bird is absent and another female feeds and cares for the nestlings, this pitch-in caregiver is likely to become the father bird's next mate. Humans operate somewhat differently, Daly and Wilson acknowledge. However, these scientists do notice that the reciprocity that grows up between a biological parent and a helpful stepparent may likewise lead to "breeding opportunities."

My own "breeding opportunity" arrived about a year into Mark's and my marriage. By then we were both past thirty-five, however, and breeding proved to be less speedy and predictable than we had imagined it would be. When we finally got a positive pregnancy test, we were thrilled—until I started bleeding two weeks later, the first sign of the miscarriage that would dash our hopes. Our pastor came to visit me in the hospital.

"It must be a comfort that it's almost Christmas," he said, fumbling for words. "Baby Jesus will be here soon." No, it's not a comfort at all, I snapped back. It's an outrage, an ugly reminder of what I long for but will never have.

The next week, Mark got a call from Bekka, his ex, Kristen's mother. She was pregnant. The pregnancy had come as a surprise, she hinted, but she and Stephen were excited, and Kristen was excited too. Mark broke the news to me gently, and we cried together again. We cried for our lost pregnancy. We cried because it seemed a real possibility that we would never be able to have a child together. And though we didn't say so, I think we also cried in fear that we might lose Kristen as well. Once she gained a little brother or sister in Minneapolis, would she become even more firmly tied to her mother's household, slipping away from ours?

Three months later, I was pregnant again.

When one adult conceives children with more than one partner, questions of inheritance, lineage, and comparative well-being are never far away. Conflicts arise, and the law steps in; this is the stuff of prenuptial agreements and custody battles. But I am more intrigued by what we might learn from the Darwinian scientists who first alerted me to my own mixed motives at the point where this issue arises for me: the intersection of stepmothering and mothering. Daly and Wilson titled the little book that first got me thinking along these lines *The Truth about Cinderella*. The truth about Cinderella, they argue, is that the stepmother desires her own children's flourishing far more than she cares for the well-being of her stepchild. The truth about Cinderella is that the stepmother is willing to oppress her, to banish her, even to kill her, if that seems to be in the interest of the children who came from her own body. The fairy tale makes that much clear. What Daly and Wilson add is a scientific explanation: animals, they argue, instinctively discriminate in favor of their own young. The "Cinderella effect"—the harm stepparents sometimes visit upon their stepchildren—is part of a stepparent's subconscious pursuit of reproductive advantage.

When one male lion displaces another as the dominant male in a pride, he systematically kills the nursing cubs of all the females who are now under his sway. Why provide food and protection for another male's cubs? Females robbed of their nurslings will go into heat sooner, making them ready to breed with him. Some primate species follow the same pattern. Daly and Wilson's research suggests that the perpetrators in such cases are usually males, though they do mention one species of tropical marsh-dwelling bird, the jacana, in which a female who displaces a rival deliberately goes about breaking the eggs of her predecessor.

When it comes right down to it, I don't buy into the completely materialist understanding of human behavior that emerges when sociobiologists emphasize the evolutionary basis of human action and emotion. At the same time, I cannot overlook the bloody impulses that so often seize members of my own species. The founding narratives of Judaism, Christianity, and Islam include a powerful story that displays this terrible dynamic. When Abraham, the patriarch of all three faith traditions, and his first wife, Sarah, cannot conceive a child, Sarah urges him to impregnate Hagar, their Egyptian servant. Abraham marries Hagar, and she gives birth to Ishmael. Competition sets in. Hagar now looks on Sarah with contempt—so enraging Sarah that she mistreats Hagar, who flees into the desert with her son. God protects the two, and they return to Abraham's camp. Later, Sarah gives birth to Isaac, and the conflict resumes. Jealous of Ishmael and eager to ensure that Abraham's wealth and blessing will go to her own son, Sarah drives Hagar and Ishmael into the desert, where Sarah knows they will be without water, food, and shelter from elements and beasts. Other jealous mothers and stepmothers have done worse. Sociologists who study crime have identified a far-ranging "Cinderella effect": children are far more likely to be killed by their stepparents than by their parents, and they are also more likely to suffer "unintentional childhood fatalities" while in a stepparent's care.

Having children of my own would bring me great joy. It would also disclose a disturbing truth. Mothering and stepmothering could come into conflict. I wanted to know the truth about Cinderella because I sensed the intrusion of a dark new temptation. I wanted to know the truth about Cinderella because I believe that acknowledging a dangerous passion is the first step in healing it.

At first, sharing my anticipation with seven-year-old Kristen added to the joy of my long-desired pregnancy. After my first ultrasound, in fact, I let her be the one to tell Mark that I was carrying not just one baby but two. Why wasn't he there to find out in person? Back then, at least in conservative towns like ours, women still labored in medical cubicles, their husbands banished to a waiting room. Likewise, Mark was not expected or invited to be present for my ultrasound—and even I was not offered a view of the screen. I had at least eight ultrasounds over the course of this high-risk pregnancy, and not once did I catch a glimpse of an arm, a leg, a head, a bottom.

On that June day, however, the technician got a good view, and what she saw was more arms, legs, heads, and bottoms than she had expected to see. She kept this discovery to herself as she bustled out to share it with some unseen collaborator. Soon my doctor entered the room. "You are carrying twins," he said.

I called Mark right away, but he didn't answer his office phone. (This was before cell phones and even before office phones had voicemail.) So I drove to my friend Eileen's house to pick up Kristen, who had been playing with Eileen's daughters while I had my appointment. Once we were back at our house, I dialed her father's office number and handed her the receiver. This time he picked up.

"We have a big surprise for you, Daddy," she proclaimed dramatically. "But you have to guess what it is!" She made him guess, and guess again, until he began to sputter with impatience. She squealed with laughter, seizing center stage. "You and Dorothy are having twins!"

That day and in the weeks that followed, Mark and I were shaken by our news, aware that major challenges lay ahead. *Two* babies? But we were also thrilled to encounter such bounty after a long period of waiting and loss. Kristen acted thrilled too, and she probably was for the moment, though we soon realized that it must have been hard for her that all the important adults in her life were preparing for the arrival of new children, when she was still so small and so uncertain about where she fit. Two parents. Two stepparents. Three infants. And her.

When Bekka went into labor that July, Mark went into high gear to get Kristen back to Minneapolis. Her mother wanted her to be in the delivery room during the birth. When Kristen, now a big sister, returned to our house a few days later, she grabbed both of my hands and locked her eyes on mine.

"Oh, Dorothy," she said with all the earnestness she could muster. "Having a baby really, really hurts! You wouldn't believe how awful it is. My mom was screaming. I don't think you should do it!" It was too late for that, of course.

There were times during the coming weeks when my pregnancy was so tenuous that it seemed once again that

Kristen's only siblings would be in Minneapolis. Shortly after Kristen's summer with us ended, I went into labor, many weeks too soon, and my doctor told Mark that our two babies would probably die. Neither man passed that warning along to me. Instead, they confined me to the hospital, where I would remain until the babies attained a viable size and our insurance company balked (amazingly, the company allowed six weeks, a stretch that would be unthinkable now). I was like a termite queen: my only purpose was to swell with offspring, my huge immobile body secreting hormones while workers scurried back and forth to bring me nourishment and keep me clean. Kristen came down twice during those weeks to visit Mark, but children were not allowed to enter the maternity ward where I was staying, so she just waved hello from the parking lot beneath my window. I ached to hug her but could not.

Our twins, Martha and John, were born in October—beautiful, healthy, and unimaginably demanding. Weeks would pass before I got two consecutive hours of sleep.

Now add to the picture a very energetic seven-year-old whom we had previously placed pretty consistently at the center of attention. When Kristen arrived for Thanksgiving break, I felt as if a tornado had blown into the house. Just as the babies drifted off to sleep, some force would impel her toward the crib they shared. "You are *so cute*," she'd say, poking a finger under one chin or the other. A cry would erupt like a shrieking siren, and I'd drag myself off the sofa to make the rescue. "Back off!" I wanted to snarl. "Stay behind the yellow tape!"

But I didn't. I was not a lion or a jacana bird. I was just an exhausted woman with too many people to love and care for all at once. Although I could not staunch my feelings, I had learned by now to watch my tongue. I walked to the crib, took Kristen's hand, and led her over to the sofa to listen to the next chapter in our book.

Fortunately, we were heading to the country to spend Thanksgiving with Kristen's rollicking band of cousins. She was excited, and Mark and I were too. Caring for two babies would surely be easier with a grandmother and two aunts on the scene to help, I assumed. When we arrived, everyone cooed and cuddled and admired the babies for an hour or so; I was happy and proud. But then our hosts returned to their cooking and games as I tried to settle the little ones into an upstairs crib. But they wouldn't settle. They fussed. They screamed. They loudly demonstrated to my Midwestern in-laws that the East Coast professional who had married into their family was not much of a mother.

Be thankful, I told myself again and again. Be thankful, I told Mark, who joined me for many long hours in the cold upstairs bedroom, rocking and patting and changing diapers until one of those rare moments when the twins, and he and I, finally slipped into brief, fretful sleep. We are thankful, we agreed, except when we are not. Mark and I felt relieved when it was time to leave, but Kristen was bereft. She suspected that the fun she had thought this holiday would hold was over. And she was (mostly) right.

That Sunday, John and Martha were baptized in our church in Valparaiso. My parents arrived for the occasion, along with two sets of godparents, the relatives with whom we had celebrated Thanksgiving, and several other friends. We set out ham, fruit, cheese, and crackers for the lunch that would follow and headed off to church. Kristen—who knew plenty about church and how to behave there—would not sit still in the pew, and when we stood to go forward for the baptism itself, she first held back and then pushed to the front, slumping sulkily and fiddling with her dress and hair. "This is boring," she said a little too loudly as the pastor placed his wet hand on Martha's head. Back in the pew, Kristen continued to whine, fussing so loudly that Mark finally left the sanctuary with her. It was all downhill from there. As friends and relatives gathered for lunch at our home, her discontent was on full display.

So we gave each other some space for a couple of hours. One of the great gifts of those years was that a family much like ours lived next door: a father, a stepmother, and Catherine, a little girl Kristen's age who visited them about as often as Kristen visited us. Mark called Catherine's dad and asked if Kristen could come over to play. Yes, that would be fine. So off she went, none too soon for us or for her, displaced again but this time in a happy way.

Kristen returned at suppertime, when all the guests but my parents had departed. As Mark greeted Kristen and asked about her afternoon—she and Catherine had a great time, she reported—I nursed the babies and put them in their crib, leaving my mother standing watch nearby. Then I joined Kristen in the kitchen.

"Popo has his video camera," I said. "How about if we film an episode of our cooking show?" Pretending that our shared work in the kitchen was being televised had been one of our favorite activities in the months before her visits got so complicated. Her face brightened, and she ran to pull our matching yellow aprons out of a drawer. Meanwhile, I searched the refrigerator for food—I needed to find ingredients for a dish Kristen would consider tasty (her enthusiasm for it must show); a dish requiring assembly and heat (though not too much); a dish that would look appealing on camera. Eureka! I pulled out three items and placed them on the counter.

Kristen and I put on our aprons and positioned my dad in the kitchen doorway with his camera. After making sure he had a good view, we declared that we were ready. He pushed the Record button, and a little red light began to glow above the lens.

"Hey good lookin', whatcha got cookin'?" we sang together, moving our hands back and forth like jazz dancers. "How about cookin' somethin' up with me?"

"Welcome to our cooking show!" Kristen exclaimed, stretching her arms toward the camera in an enthusiastic gesture of hospitality. "We haven't been on for a long time because Dorothy here has two new twins. But I have a new children's cookbook, so today we are going to cook something from there. We are going to make a *very* scrumptious dish. It is *very* easy, and it is *very* good for babies and children. We are going to make little pizzas!"

I announced the ingredients: "For this dish, we will use English muffins for the crust (Kristen held one up before the camera), tomato sauce (likewise), and cheese." The cheese would make the pizza look good and taste good, she added, displaying that item as well, and declaring it "*very* nutritious." The ingredients now stood in a perfect row. Ta-da! The camera swept across them.

"Kristen will read the instructions from the cookbook," I said, "and I'll do what they say."

"I have to do it too," she reminded me sternly. She'd be watching to make sure I didn't do it all myself; I was just the sous-chef. She picked up the open book. I placed my hands on her slender shoulders and rotated her body to face the camera.

Setting the English muffin halves onto the toaster oven tray was the first step. Once they were in place, Kristen handed me the book, climbed onto a stool to reach the counter, and smeared sauce on each half. She found the next step—grating the cheese—"a little bit boring," so I did that while she presented a commercial.

"This is a *very* useful microwave," she announced, gesturing toward the appliance as if she were a model on a television game show. This "*very* useful" microwave had a light and a clock, each of which was also "*very* useful." Best of all, she enthused, we had gotten this microwave for a "*very* cheap price." Meanwhile, off camera, my infant twins were lustily declaring that they were ready for their next meal, and my body was responding. As I grated the cheese, milk began to soak through the front of my sweater. I fought to retain my focus on the show.

As soon as the commercial wrapped, I put my hand on Kristen's shoulder and guided her back to her stool by the counter. I needed, and my twins needed, to keep this show moving. I picked up the cookbook and forged ahead. "Sprinkle the grated cheese on top of the pizza," I read.

At this point, a louder cry in the background interrupted the show. Martha and John had been making noise for a while, but this outburst was different. It came from my mother.

"Dorothy, they're starving! You've got to feed them!"

"Now the pizzas will go into the toaster oven for a while," Kristen, heedless, announced to our imaginary audience.

"It sounds like some other food is needed too," I whispered into her ear.

She turned her eyes to me and spoke softly, sadly, and with utter firmness: "You can't go."

I slid the tray of little pizzas into the toaster oven and pressed the lever.

"How long?" my mother wailed.

"A couple of minutes," I whispered in reply.

For Kristen, these two remaining minutes presented an opening for another commercial. As she pitched a colorful hot pad to her television audience, the phone rang. It was my grandmother. My mother, bless her, said we'd call back soon, and my father, bless him, did not put down his camera. We were almost to the finish line, and the crowd roared . . . no, wait, that was the sound of hangry twins wanting to be fed. Kristen and I finished our performance with flair, jazz hands fluttering beside our smiling faces as we sang.

"How about cookin' somethin' up with me—Yeah!"

The videotape my father shot that evening is one of our most cherished possessions. Kristen's theatrical gifts were beginning to show, and if I may say so, my ability to adapt in the kitchen was also on display. Over the years, we showed this tape to each of Kristen's boyfriends, howling with laughter as we viewed her precocious performance.

That's the pretty account of the cooking show that is lodged in our family's shared memory.

But for me, the scene is more complicated. When I watch it now, what I notice are all the voices competing for my attention on the night of my children's baptism. My twins are screaming. My mother is pleading with me to feed them. And Kristen is saying, "You can't go."

Almost every parent will recognize the feeling of being overwhelmed I experienced during that long Thanksgiving weekend, and most will be able to imagine how much the demands of infant twins might aggravate that parental sense of anxiety and despair. And I understand that a formerly-only-child seven-year-old in a similar situation could be demanding even if the family were not a stepfamily. Such moments are familiar and mildly challenging in families of every kind.

Still, situations like this one can feel a little different to a stepmother.

"You can't go," the child says.

"You go all the time," the stepmother thinks but cannot say.

She, the stepmother, must be on, ready to parent, whenever the child shows up. Moreover, she must be able, emotionally, to expand and contract on demand the rhythms of her household—and also, more important, the capacities of her heart. It's not that the child doesn't also have to make difficult emotional maneuvers. I'm simply calling attention to the distinctive challenges experienced by one of the adults on the scene, because this adult matters for her own sake—and because this particular adult's capacity to understand and deal with her feelings may have great influence, one way or another, on the harmony of all concerned.

Such challenges come as part of a bargain I have found well worth making, even though there was a rough spell around the time two underweight infants were added to the mix. For many other stepmothers, dealing with conflicting feelings, and with actual conflicts, becomes a source of ongoing anguish and, sometimes, grief.

5

THE UGLY WORD

From its origins in Old English and related Germanic languages, the word *stepmother* has been tinged with grief. At the root of *step* is *astieped*, "bereaved." A *steopbearn* was a child whose parent had died; a *steopmodor* was the woman who stepped in to care for the child, often after marrying the child's father. In the centuries before divorce became widely available, women became stepmothers because death came first. Death also came often, especially to women, who underwent the dangers of childbirth in septic conditions and without the help of antibiotics, surgery, and other modern boons.

Because there have always been bereaved children, there have always been women who took up the tasks of caring for *steopbearns* in one way or another. Patterns have varied. Among the Indigenous peoples of North America, for example, tribal groups typically absorbed the orphans of their deceased members. In the villages of the premodern West, bereaved fathers sometimes found new partners, but bereaved children might instead be taken into relatives' homes, sent out as apprentices, or placed in monastic communities. And it's important to note the sad fact, across time and place, that some children have not been provided with any refuge at all, trying to make their own way as best they can.

Changes that began to imbue the role of stepmother with features that remain familiar in white, middle-class America came with the rise of the nuclear family in the early modern period. As cities grew and a money economy took hold, many households came increasingly to be centered on a married couple and their children. In the nuclear families of the rising European middle class, the man and the woman comprising this couple performed different duties, but both were indispensable to the household's well-being. Children had duties too, especially in agricultural or less privileged families, but as modern patterns emerged and prosperity increased, so did a growing sense that childhood was a less productive stage of life meant primarily for play and personal development. This stage of life was meant to be enjoyed under the watchful eye of a loving mother. In America, this family form—a forerunner of the

Dad-and-Mom-and-Dick-and-Jane model that would briefly grab national attention some centuries later—belonged primarily to relatively well-off immigrants from Europe. The idealization of childhood and motherhood that underwrote this pattern did not apply to less privileged children and mothers, step or not. No ideal of nurturing family relationships was upheld by those who had power over the many mothers and children enslaved, separated, and abused in the Western Atlantic world. And yet nurturing relationships often developed, as women within the community of the enslaved stepped up to care for bereaved enslaved children as well as they possibly could.

In one of the few well-researched books on the history of stepfamilies, Lisa Wilson describes the experience of stepmothers and stepchildren in early American families of European descent. In the towns of colonial New England, the death of a wife and mother created a void in a household that made its smooth functioning nearly impossible. Thus widowers were under heavy pressure to provide a "new mother" for their children. The correspondence of a Puritan minister, Thomas Clap, provides a window into this common situation. After his wife, Mary, died in childbirth in 1737, friends and family members frequently urged Clap to find a new wife for his seven children's sake, as Mary herself had urged him to do from her deathbed. Many widowers remarried within a year, but Clap was too sorrowful to go courting. Finally, after a difficult three years during which he relied for help on servants and relatives, Clap decided to look for a wife. "I have now a Family to take care of and none can act the woman's part in it, so well as one that acts in the Relation & Capacity of Wife," he wrote in his journal. He was deeply aware of how important it was to choose wisely, and he fretted about the possibility of choosing an "angry, Fretful" woman who would cause "Jarring or Discord" in his household. His prayer was for a virtuous woman of faith who would "love my children for my sake, and wisely and carefully Educate and Govern them with the Authority and Tenderness of a natural Parent." He finally married a wealthy widow with six children of her own.

A couple of decades later, back in what Anglo-American colonists called "the mother country," Samuel Johnson's path-breaking dictionary of the English language offered a definition of *stepmother* suitable to Thomas Clap's situation: "It seems to mean, in the mind of those who use it, a woman who has *stepped* into the vacant place of the true mother." And indeed, during this period, family members did generally view a second (or third, or fourth) wife as a replacement mother, often accepting her presence in their lives as natural and good in spite of grief for her predecessor. And she might, without apology or shame, find this description an agreeable one. Sarah Woolsey, a Massachusetts stepmother who embraced this understanding of her role, signed letters to her stepchildren "your truly affectionate Mother."

Notice, however, that Johnson's definition also includes a word that calls Sarah Woolsey's positive attitude into question: she was not and never would be the "true" mother. Even though functioning without the contributions of stepmothers was difficult for bereaved families, suspicion of such women was widespread. Some suspicion was rooted in the folk tales of earlier centuries; "wicked" stepmothers were already stock characters in the popular imagination. In addition, the negative stereotype articulated reasonable worries that still plague those whose fathers remarry. What would this mean for a household's economy and children's inheritance? Would a father's new wife be—as "Step Mother England" was viewed by rebellious colonists during the American Revolution—a self-centered, older authority figure who exploited the children she had in her power?

Stepmothers were in a deeply contradictory and potentially painful situation. On the one hand, they were indispensable to the well-being of countless middle-class families. On the other hand, they were suspect as inadequate and perhaps immoral imitations of what was really needed: a True Mother. "Mother" was rapidly becoming an idealized figure in the sentiments of nineteenth-century Americans.

Mothers were, are, and have been crucial figures for children and for society in every age, to be sure—but few, in any period, have been the naturally virtuous, utterly nurturing, unfailingly selfless Angels of the Home that mothers in general were held up to be in the popular magazines, novels, and images of that day. And when one of these beatific creatures died, she was likely to seem more angelic still.

Part of the cultural ideology undergirding this notion of the angelic mother, however, was a notion of "true womanhood" that might also be applied to a woman who had not given birth—provided that her heart was loving and pure. Stepmothers who met this criterion deserved some respect, a few reformers declared. In the years before the Civil War, when movements for reform flooded the northern states, such reformers drew on the romantic image of women to combat prejudice against stepmothers, in the interest of justice to them and harmony in families. Popular magazines and books sympathetically acknowledged the difficult duties stepmothers performed—"without the authority of a mother, yet with all a mother's responsibility"—and painted didactic portraits of virtuous women who were able to love other women's children with a full and womanly heart.

An 1849 story in *Mothers' Journal and Family Visitant* provides a good example. The story begins with a bereaved sister and brother who commiserate about their father's new wife. "I just went into mother's chamber, and it seemed as if I could see her beautiful pale face pressing the pillow," the brother says, "and I thought how kind, how good, how like an angel she was to all of us; and now to have that ugly old maid here." As the story unfolds, however, the stepmother proves again and again that she is kind and tender, and the children realize that their initial scorn was mistaken. When the stepdaughter begs for forgiveness, the fictional stepmother grants it readily, humbly revealing additional depths of virtue. The girl's initial resistance had been "natural," she says, "for your own mother was an angel compared to me." No, the girl gushes; the two are "sister angels—one in heaven and one on earth."

Somehow (imagine!), fiction like this did not overpower cultural prejudice against stepmothers. However, the same age of reform that attempted this makeover also led to changes in society and law that would ultimately create an alternate pathway into stepmotherhood, a pathway that did not require a mother's death. As women gained access to education and employment outside the home, they also gradually won increased rights to control their property and to maintain custody of their children when their husbands proved unworthy. Reformers also fought for the legal right to divorce for those caught in oppressive and damaging relationships. By the 1890s, divorce was legal throughout the United States, though still rare. A century later, divorce had become relatively easy to obtain and, indeed, a widely accepted element of how Americans make, unmake, and remake our family systems.

Although stepmothers like the second Mrs. Clap and her successors in nineteenth-century America were typically chosen by widowers to be replacement mothers, twenty-first-century women usually become stepmothers not because a mother has died but because a child's family has suffered a death of a different kind. Whether our new spouses are widowed or divorced, however, we have most likely connected with them because of our qualities as their companions and their qualities as ours, not because of children's needs. In most cases, including my own, the "true" mother is still on the scene; in others, she is present in memory and imagination. What each woman is called—stepmother, mother, or something else—somehow reflects on the status of the other.

The word *stepmother* creates distance between an adult and a child even while signaling that they are related to each other in a lasting and intimate bond. It surges in two directions at once, creating currents amid whose force everyone concerned must navigate, on seas that are widely acknowledged to be stormy ones. Fairy tales explore the depths of these seas, and even high-brow authors noted for their wisdom and compassion sometimes sail there. In his most influential book, Enlightenment philosopher Immanuel Kant says that "stepmotherly nature" deprives some people of the resources needed to live well in the world. In Leo Tolstoy's *Anna Karenina*, a woman who complains that the children of the household are given too much privilege meets this rebuke: "Anyone who didn't know you would think you were not a mother but a stepmother." And even Pope Francis, usually a spokesperson and exemplar of mercy, insults stepmothers in a speech meant, ironically, to commend forgiveness and forbearance. The model the church needs to follow, the pope declared in 2015, "is that of a mother who does not send away her children; that would make her a stepmother."

In each case, the word's structure invites comparison to another woman whose situation is assumed to be more secure, important, and beneficent. "Mother" is there, in the root. But an actual mother is not there, in the person.

"You're not my mother! You're my stepmother!" a ten-year-old screams at his father's new wife in the movie *Stepmom*. Ben knows that his words—and one word in particular—will draw blood. He has hurled a weapon. He has voiced rejection. He has cast his lot with a woman who is not present, hoping thereby to overthrow the tyranny of the woman he is stuck with whenever he visits his father. On the surface, what's at stake is a minor disciplinary matter: his stepmother has asked him to put his dishes in the sink. But he knows, and she knows, that more than that is going on between them.

Ben's remark reminds me of that time I said something similar to the white-haired gentleman in the mountain village. "I'm not her mother, I'm her stepmother," I said, reversing Ben's phrase. The man had assumed I was Kristen's mother; Kristen found his remark confusing; I tried to clarify. I meant no harm, and I was not voicing rejection. Still, saying the ugly word out loud created pain in all three of us. Kristen burst into tears. The man shuffled sadly away. And I suddenly realized how vulnerable I was in this role, this relationship.

Forty years ago, a woman I know married a man with two preschoolers. The children's mother, who had abandoned them, remained a presence at the margins of their lives, though sometimes she did not show up for years at a time. The stepmother was their constant caregiver and, with her husband, their faithful parent. The kids called her "Mommy," then "Mom" as they grew older, and their schools, friends, and doctors considered her their mother.

Recently the woman who had given them birth died. The daughter, now in her forties, called with the news. "Mom, my mother has died!" she cried. My friend was hurt and confused. Hadn't she been the mother, in every way that counts? She could hear and appreciate "Mom"—but what was with "my mother"?

Another acquaintance of mine, the thirty-something stepmother of a seven-year-old boy, was devastated when her stepson asked her to help him buy a gift for his "real" mother. Many stepmothers have found the word *real* to be a slap in the face. My own slap in the face arrived in reverse, when the white-haired gentleman in the mountain village mistook me for a "real" mother when I was not.

Confusion about the words used to describe family relationships can prove troubling to anyone who belongs to a family constituted by any means other than genetic transfer within a heterosexual marriage. This has long been an issue in families shaped by adoption, for example. Although law and society grant adoptive mothers all the rights and responsibilities of motherhood, others sometimes use words that diminish their maternal standing. This can hurt, even when adoptive mothers are themselves clear and confident in their role. "Language signals that adoption is 'other' and, often, inferior," writes historian and adoptive mother

Barbara Melosh. Each of the many terms that salt everyday talk about parentage—*natural, real, adoptive, biological, their own*—carries nuance, subtly assessing the quality and character of life-shaping relationships.

Words matter.

Since starting to read about stepfamilies, I have been astonished by the range of words people throw around within and about them—and also by the passion with which these words are thrown. In *Stepmonster*, one of the most popular books on being a female stepparent, Wednesday Martin rages about the negative attitudes she feels she must constantly absorb, especially from her stepchildren but also from other people. It's enough to make her feel and act, she writes, like the monster they take her to be! Martin believes that most stepmothers, including herself, do not want the kids who came along with their new spouses. Quite different is Barbara Waterman, a Jungian psychoanalyst who had yearned for children throughout a failed marriage and years of infertility. Waterman found immense satisfaction in becoming a stepmother in her forties. The role, she enthuses, allowed her to fulfill her archetypal female identity and ushered her into a rhapsodic experience of "Motherhood." Having a child, even if part-time, was for her such a satisfying experience that she dropped the *step* from *stepmother* and capitalized the remaining part of the word, signaling her joy at having attained full womanly identity as Mother. These two women's identical legal relationships to their husbands' children became two utterly different things as a result of their very different personalities and experiences. The words they chose in writing about their lives articulated that difference.

The list of available words is long; together they create numerous nuances that add up to a compendium of interpretations and assessments. In their comprehensive textbook about stepfamilies, sociologists Lawrence Ganong and Marilyn Coleman list the terms they have seen used for such families in academic and professional literature: "reconstituted, blended, reconstructed, reorganized, reformed, recycled, combined, rem, step-, second-time around, merged, and remarried families." The terms applied to stepparents are equally varied: "non-parents, half-parents, acquired parents, added parents, and second or third parents" and, more recently, "sociological parents." (Here's a clever one: the child of a gay father called her dad's new husband her "vice dad.") Ganong and Coleman, who are influential scholars in this field, settle on *step-* (family, parent, father, mother, child). Against scholars who argue that step-words carry negative cultural resonance, Ganong and Coleman think these terms confer more advantages than the alternatives do. (*Reconstituted* sounds like orange juice, they suggest, and *blended* reminds them of whiskey, in addition to being somewhat unclear—does it refer to all stepfamilies or just to those where both adults bring children from past relationships?)

Kirsti Cole and Valerie R. Renegar, scholars of language as well as stepmothers themselves, disagree. Cultural associations with the word *stepmother* are so negative that trying to rehabilitate the term is hopeless, they conclude after researching the use of the ugly word in online discussions among stepmothers. Even when stepmothers distance themselves from the stereotype—"I'm not wicked," they say—the ugly word survives in the shadows, its value diminished by the culture's exaltation of biological motherhood. Cole and Renegar argue that "an alternative term should capture the importance of the role, its level of responsibility, and the unique nature of this close-caring relationship, while also avoiding competition with biological mothers." In their own families, they have settled on possessive forms of their personal names: the stepkids say "My Kirsti" or "My Val."

The apparently harmless word that most frequently complicates the situation is *blended. Blended* is a popular term, I suspect, because it suggests a positive outcome to the family's story without acknowledging brokenness or falling into the shadow of the troubling term *step. Blended* does not identify certain family members as outsiders or transients but presumes that all are equally well integrated. It smooths out discord and difficulties, implying that everything is now just fine. The "blended" family is just one kind of family among many, the term implies, and indeed this family is one in which relational success has been attained and differences have been reconciled. To judge from the prominence of blended family terminology in popular therapeutic and self-help literature, these are probably families in which the parents have had a "good divorce" and the kids have avoided harm because they got counseling.

"Divorce happy-talk" like this is designed to make adults feel better, insists Elizabeth Marquardt, the author of a study of children of divorce. Marquardt, whose parents divorced when she was four, argues that our culture almost never acknowledges children's perspectives on divorce, which leaves a mark not only on those obviously damaged by family dissolution but also on many who are successful by the usual educational, professional, and personal measures. Drawing on her own experience and that of hundreds of interviewees, Marquardt contrasts her subjects' stories of loss with the general acceptance of divorce she perceives in the wider culture. Most of what is said publicly about this situation is what adults want to hear, she asserts: there are many kinds of families today, she hears people saying, so "we should embrace family diversity and stop making divorced parents feel bad." Contrary to Marquardt's generalization, I do embrace diverse family forms, and I believe that shaming people who belong to one kind or another helps neither children nor adults. People are free to describe their families however they see fit. At the same time, I agree with Marquardt that it's ultimately life giving to acknowledge the wrongs and wounds woven into our family stories, even if doing so makes adults "feel bad." Embracing family diversity while also speaking of these hard things attends to our children's feelings and acknowledges what they know to be true. Honesty is also helpful in the healing we adults need.

Only after I became a stepmother did I understand the profound work of words like these. What we call each other and what we hear others call us define who we are to each other in ways that don't simply *reflect* our relationships. What we call each other can actually *shape* our relationships.

From the beginning, Kristen called me "Dorothy." No problem there. It was a different matter, one day, when she called her father "Mark." She was simply copying me; I found it weird to call my boyfriend "Daddy," even when speaking to her. But I could tell at once that hearing "Mark" in her little voice horrified him. The divorce was painfully altering his position in Kristen's world. While he knew that he was her father and always would be, he desperately desired assurance that she knew this too. So I instantly shifted to calling him "Daddy" whenever I was speaking to her. She never wavered again in her use of this name for him. Before long, using it did not feel weird to me either.

Asking my stepchild to call me "Mom"—a request other stepmothers sometimes make—was not an option I ever considered; it was always clear that that name was already taken. That said, I admit I have always been pleased when Kristen says "my parents" in a way that includes me and her stepfather. (In my humble opinion, both of us have earned this after many years of active care for her.) And I have felt hurt when she or others have referred to Bekka and Stephen as her parents, as if Mark and I do not exist. I once heard a neighbor of theirs ask Kristen where her parents were. It was a casual question, no issues of identity involved; this man simply needed to know Bekka and Stephen's whereabouts in that moment and had no idea of who the people Kristen was standing with—Mark and me—were. This kind of casual reference must have happened all the time as she was growing up, going to school from their house, being part of their Minneapolis community. To that world, *in* that world, her mother and stepfather probably appeared to be her parents, her only parents. But to Kristen, they were Mom and Stephen, not Mom and Dad, or so I've been told.

For me, the bigger question has been what *I* should call *her*. Context matters. Perhaps I could have fudged things a little that afternoon in the mountain village; I could have attempted to change the subject, for example. That might have defused the situation, but I was so eager to address Kristen's perplexity about what the man had said that this ploy did not occur to me. Besides, friends of her mother are plentiful in the community that gathers in that village, and I certainly would not have wanted Bekka to hear that I was masquerading as Kristen's mother. That said, there have been a few other occasions when I have allowed this misperception to stand—among strangers at a store or amusement park, for example, or when clarifying our relationship would only introduce an irrelevant distinction, singling her out in front of a group of teenaged peers who really don't care which adult is which if only we'd all just leave them alone.

In general, I have defended clarity, though this strategy sometimes requires improvisation. Do you have any children? Yes, I could say from the beginning. (The ambiguity of *you* in English—it can be singular or plural—comes in handy here. The plural *we* is helpful too; I couldn't claim this child on my own, but I could seize a share of my husband's valid claim.) What was more difficult—and what still feels complicated—is the word *mine*. The possessive pronoun isn't such a problem if a family term does not follow it. In our early years together, I often called Kristen "my little girl" in casual public conversation, which felt fine; and when Mark and I were together, she could be "our daughter." But she was never simply "mine." This may seem obvious, but it actually involved tiptoeing across a verbal tightrope. It was important not to violate the truth, anger her mother, or confuse Kristen by claiming her too boldly—but at the same time, Mark and I would never want to deny, through our words, that she really did belong with us and to us during the times she was in our care.

Looking back, I wonder if there was some cost to all this clarity, some loss built into my repeated declarations that "she is not my daughter" and "I am not her mother." Don't get me wrong: I know who is who. (Even after all these years, it feels important to keep that in mind and to say it aloud.) But now I wonder what might have been different if I had let a little more light shine through that wall of words.

The terms by which steprelatives address one another, a recent study found, become ways of expressing distance or closeness, formality or informality; these words articulate the rules and roles of belonging. For example, a child who refuses to call his stepmother "Mom" may be guarding his independence, a move that makes lots of sense depending on the age of the child and his loyalty to his mother. Maybe the parallel refusal—not calling a child "mine"—has a similar effect. Might I have hoped that these verbal fences would guard some independence of my own? Or were these fences creating obstacles to closeness in ways I did not intend and could not see?

Loss acknowledged clears space for what is new in a way that "happy talk" cannot. One of the most powerful stories in which the gift of new family is given and received is set at the foot of Jesus's cross, as the story is written in Christian Scriptures. As Jesus dies, he sees the grief of those who think they are losing him forever. No happy talk is possible. But for those who love him enough to stay with him in that terrible moment, the possibility of new relationship opens wide. Seeing his mother and the disciple he loves standing together, Jesus gives them to one another in a new way. "Woman, here is your son," he says to Mary, and to the disciple he says, "Here is your mother." A new family is formed, and the relational words are simple and clear. Son. Mother. The Gospel text records that "from that hour the disciple took her into his own home."

Perhaps this kind of relationship—a friend and a mother united after the death of someone they both love—is seen as too different from creating a new family after divorce to provide any inspiration. But considering different possibilities than those of one's own cultural context can open new lines of vision as we try to discern how nurture and relationship can be renewed after loss.

In this book, where I am delving into something very intimate for me, I tend to emphasize what I know personally—the experience of middle-class women in a society where families are most often disrupted and refashioned through processes of divorce and remarriage. In this context, the words *mother* and *stepmother* make a certain kind of sense. In many other contexts, including some in neighborhoods near my home, different patterns of meaning and family formation exist, as do different ways of talking about them. Considering these may shed a different kind of light, and provide insight into a different kind of wisdom, on the varieties of parenting people in every neighborhood are experiencing in one way or another these days.

"I gave birth to one child, a son," Maya Angelou wrote in *Letter to My Daughter*, a book she wrote in the last years of her life. "But I have thousands of daughters. You are Black and

White. Jewish and Muslim, Asian, Spanish-speaking, Native American and Aleut. You are fat and thin and pretty and plain, gay and straight, educated and unlettered, and I am speaking to you all. Here is my offering to you." On the pages that follow, Angelou writes to all these daughters, sharing wisdom drawn from her own life.

When I read this aging Black writer's wide embrace of her readers as daughters, I appreciated it as a generous expression of affection and regard, though at first I couldn't see how these lovely words were grounded in motherhood. Reading these words again, I wonder if Angelou's use of *daughters* is related to the tradition in some Black communities of calling certain respected women *Mothers*, regardless of family or legal ties. As womanist scholar Cheryl Townsend Gilkes has shown, the term *Mother* is sometimes used to honor the life-giving leadership and nurture provided by a beloved older woman, notably in church but also in a wider community.

Another term used in some Black communities—*other mother*—also grants recognition and esteem to women who hold important roles in the lives of youngsters. The concept of "other mother"—though already long in use—was first defined academically by Patricia Hill Collins in her influential 1991 book, *Black Feminist Thought*. Collins described patterns of communal care for children by women in the

African American community that created a practice of shared support and resistance on behalf of the next generation. In Collins's account, such communal care was strong in part because it was adaptive, sustained by "constantly renegotiated relationships that African American women experience with one another, with black children, with the larger African community, and with self."

A study by Deidre Hill Butler, a scholar and stepmother who is African American, begins to make the connections between stepmothering and other mothering that intrigued me. If research on stepmothers is scarce, research on African American stepmothers is even scarcer, but Butler's 2005 interviews and online survey provide a good starting point. As Collins's claim that other mothering was widespread in Black communities would predict, most of the African American stepmothers who responded to Butler's questions reported that they figured out how to be stepmothers partly by drawing on their experience in communities where several women pitched in to raise children. "When I was growing up, every woman on the street, as well as my parents' female friends and female relatives, were a sort of 'mother,'" one recounted. "I brought that attitude into my role as stepmother." Butler sees in this and many other responses the prevalence of an "ethic of other mothering" that African

American stepmothers find supportive as they fulfill their role. For these women, what stepmothers do has precedent and does not seem abnormal. As another respondent put it, "The concept of women coming together to rear children is very typical in our culture."

That said, many problems similar to those experienced by white stepmothers also affect Butler's subjects—negative cultural stereotypes, disappointed expectations of instant connection with their stepchildren, and ambiguity about what this role requires of them. It's interesting that another 2005 study of kinship patterns in a Black urban neighborhood also discovered a great deal of collaborative parenting among female kin and friends. In addition, however, the researchers discovered that almost none of the women studied were willing to provide care for the children their partners had fathered with other women. Even though other mothering can be an asset within many African American stepfamilies, this dynamic can be complicated by the fact that being the generous partner of a man who has made a baby with someone else can be just plain hard. (Possibly this speculation arises only from my sensitivity to stepmothering issues. The study doesn't explore the reasons for declining the opportunity to help.)

I deeply respect the matriarchal web that strengthens cultures where other mothering is honored. And I'm sadly aware of the relative absence of a communal maternal web where I live. My own family is shaped by the kinship patterns of privileged white culture. Even so, this new term—*other mother*—helps me to see the world in a new way. This term also reminds me of a more general anthropological concept: *allomother*. This word refers to the parental-type attention given by females across cultures (and even across species) to youngsters who are not their biological offspring. Today, most families rely on lots of allocare—stepmothers, yes, but also babysitters, day care workers, teachers, grandmothers, neighbors, aunts, and more. This is how we improvise and how families change.

Throughout many cultures, across racial and ethnic lines, many women "mother" young people. If you go to my own predominantly white church on Mother's Day, you'll hear prayers and praise for "all the people who gave us birth, cared for us, helped us along the way, and mothered us to maturity." Ask some questions, and you'll learn that many of the women in the room do not fit the normative pattern of biological, residential, lifelong female nurture implied by "mother" in our middle-class context. At the same time, you'll sense that most of these women have provided generous care for youngsters in different ways. The more inclusive prayer represents an effort to recognize and honor these women, a gesture I and many others who sit in these pews deeply affirm.

Greeting card companies are beginning to recognize and thank the many kinds of people who guide and care for those who are younger than themselves. My local Target displays a rack full of these specialty items each spring. "With Love to someone who's been like a Mom to me," proclaims the flowered cover of one card. Another has a simpler cover but a more complicated thought: "On Mother's Day, we think about the women who make a difference in our lives, the ones who want the best for us, the ones who keep on caring, no matter what." These cards might be appropriate for some stepmothers, though none of the cards on the rack I'm examining uses that word.

While I affirm such general recognition of the many nurturers children rely on, it's still important to me to come to terms with the particular kind of allomother I am in relation to just one specific person. This person, Kristen, is a woman bereaved by her parent's divorce; a woman who has a good mother who is not me; a woman who is infinitely dear to her father, my husband; a woman whom I have known and loved for decades.

In spite of the shadows cast by the ugly word, I appreciate the clarity that comes with considering this woman my stepdaughter and myself her stepmother. Ironically, the shadows that hover around the word *stepmother* are, for me, among its benefits. This is not divorce happy talk. Even in the twenty-first century, the prefix *step-* signals that death has come first—the death of a parent or the death of a marriage that was once generative enough to produce a child. In this way, the word honors the child's heritage and experience. And it also serves me well.

Stepmother includes *mother*, acknowledging the care I provide to my stepchild. By adding *step*, the word also reminds me that I am not the mother of the particular one to whom I am giving that care. I am one step removed. This is something I have needed to remember, even when I'd rather not. My husband, Kristen's father, is the one who bridges the short distance between us. Step-words speak our truth and recall our history. Likewise, even while acknowledging that "step" terms carry some negative connotations, noted stepfamiliy therapist Patricia Papernow also chooses to use them, in part because the word *stepfamily* "accurately reflects the step-by-step process by which step relationships are best built."

When the white-haired gentleman on the patio assumed I was Kristen's mother, I was thrilled, at first, to be perceived in that way. I was deeply into my maternal fantasies that afternoon. His comment jolted me out of those fantasies, unbalancing me and puzzling Kristen. Suddenly I had to figure out why he was calling me by a name that had never been mine, though I longed for it. And I also had to summon up and communicate clarity about who did own that name, as Mark and I had agreed was best for Kristen. I wonder now what Kristen would have said to the man if she had tried to explain who I was. Possibly Daddy's wife or Daddy's friend. Or maybe just Dorothy, on whom a special status had been conferred whose meaning was yet to be determined.

In spite of all the uncertainty of that moment, I appreciate what she did in fact do. She turned to me for help. A question shone from her eyes, and I was able to answer it. With that answer, Kristen started to figure out who I was: her stepmother, or as she usually says now, her stepmom. And I started to figure out what that complicated title, now claimed as my own, would mean for me as well.

6

HUNGER

Deep in a forest, a witch builds a house of bread. The roof is made of cake, the windows of spun sugar. Two lost children, famished after three days of wandering in the woods, discover the house and begin to devour it. The witch—a kind old woman, they think at first—comes out of the house and invites them in for a wonderful meal of milk and pancakes with sugar, apples, and nuts. After supper, she tucks them into cozy little beds made up with soft white sheets. Then she looks down on their rosy cheeks. *They will make a tasty morsel*, she thinks. She has built the house of bread just to lure them inside.

Visions of sugarplums had been dancing in my head for weeks: the two of us would create an adorable little house and display it in the front window for Mark, visiting relatives, and all the neighbors to see. Now we had prepared all the ingredients and set them out on the table. A tin-foiled tray—the base. Six rectangles of sturdy gingerbread, trimmed precisely to size. Gumdrops in five colors, pepper-mint sticks, and licorice, both red and black. A bowl of white icing to use as mortar. A charming fairy tale was about to come to life in my kitchen.

"Okay, here we go!" I said, squirting a thick line of icing from the pointy linen pastry bag. "The piece with the door goes here." Kristen, now ten years old, settled the base of one of the gingerbread rectangles into the icing and held on tight, steadying it, willing it to stand up straight. It didn't.

We needed reinforcement. I grabbed two cans of Campbell's tomato soup from the cupboard and set them like buttresses against the wobbling wall. "There!"

Her hands free, Kristen popped a purple gumdrop into her mouth.

"Can I do the icing?" she asked. She tossed her blonde braids over her shoulders, picked up the bag, and laid down another thick line. This time I steadied the wall, holding it at a right angle to the one held up by the soup cans. It wobbled too.

"Uh oh, I think we forgot something," I said, lifting wall number two off its foundation. "See if you can put icing down the edge where the two walls come together." Kristen scrunched her mouth as she very, very carefully positioned the tip of the pastry bag and squeezed, starting at the top and moving slowly down. She did well, but the icing, already puddling on the tinfoiled ground, was faster than she was. This mortar of mine was not up to the job. It sure was tasty though. Kristen dipped a finger into the icing and put it in her mouth. I did too.

"Maybe we should just eat everything!" I said as cheerfully as I could manage, in spite of my discouragement. She took an orange gumdrop and laughed.

After she was in bed that night, I poured myself a drink and made a stiff new batch of icing. Alone now in the night kitchen, I laid down the icing, placed and propped the walls, and prayed that they would stand. When I finally went to bed, the walls and roof were in place. Every surface in the kitchen was sticky, but I'd worry about that tomorrow, after Kristen and I had decorated the gingerbread house together.

A little over two hundred years ago, Jacob and Wilhelm Grimm hiked around the German countryside collecting the tales people told their children beside their humble hearths. The Grimm brothers were scholars intrigued by a distinctive cultural heritage they thought might be slipping away, but soon the tales they had meant merely to preserve became wildly popular, far beyond their rustic origins. And so they have remained, with Grimm stories like "Hansel and Gretel," "Snow White," and "Cinderella" ("Aschenputtel" to the Germans) told and retold in countless books and films. The tales continue to fascinate scholars too, who discern in them the unsettling dynamics of children's perilous interactions with the adult world. Some of the most dangerous of these interactions feature stepmothers.

In the Grimms' original version of the tale about the gingerbread house, Hansel and Gretel, the children in the story, are the son and daughter of a woodcutter who lives by the edge of the forest with his wife, their mother. Famine is upon the land, and the little family is down to its last loaf of bread. The wife tells the husband that they must get rid of the children, lest all four of them starve. After a little weak resistance, he agrees, and the adults lead the children deep into the woods, leaving them there to starve or be eaten by wild beasts. Hansel's cleverness enables the children to find their way home, but on the adults' second attempt, the abandonment is accomplished.

By the time the seventh edition of the Grimms' tales was published in 1857, the mother in the story had been transformed into a stepmother. Maria Tatar, a professor of German literature who has spent her career studying folk tales, concludes that as their books gained popularity, the brothers edited out the disturbing image of a mother who deliberately condemns her children to death. That a step-mother would act in this way could evidently be imagined with far less distress.

Another aspect of Hansel and Gretel's desperate situation also attracts Tatar's notice. What if the entire family of four really would have starved if the adults had not been willing to sacrifice the children? Sometimes—including in the countryside visited by the Grimms—there truly is not enough food to go around. Hunger is real, urgent, life-threatening. "Children in fairy tales live perpetually under the double threat of starvation and cannibalism," Tater writes. The threat is not an empty one; throughout history, some parents really have abandoned their children, and certain species of animals eat their own young. Adults occasionally joke with children along these lines—"You look good enough to eat," they say, or "Grrr, I'm going to eat you up." This is just a figure of speech, it may appear, but Tatar wonders about the effect. In such play, "adults may be exorcising a child's fears of being devoured, but they may also be fueling them."

To be clear, no one in our extended stepfamily has come close to eating the flesh of anyone else. And no one has ever abandoned Kristen to starvation and wild beasts. Still, grim dynamics occasionally came into play. The adults on whom she initially depended withdrew from her the shelter of a steady home built by the same love that had brought her into the world. And I, an adult who came later into her life, have been tempted to consume her presence to promote my own self-esteem and well-being, not hers.

In every family, questions about how to allocate resources arise. Who do you love more? Why does he get the drumstick? How come she gets Grandma's jewelry? In situations where love and food are plentiful, most of us muddle through and work things out—though not before a doubt or two about whether we're getting all we deserve is lodged deep in our subconscious. While it may seem that such questions belong only to childhood—and surely they do begin there—I believe they persist all our lives long.

The adult characters in fairy tales cast these passions into sharp relief. The queen who holds Snow White's fate in her hands cannot bear the girl's possessing more beauty than she does. Cinderella's stepmother wants one of her own daughters—not Cinderella—to win the hand of the prince. The woodcutter's wife wants to increase her own chance of survival in a time of want, even if it means abandoning two children to die in the forest.

Questions about how to allocate resources arise in every culture too. In some, lactating women casually and routinely nurse one another's children. If breasts are full and children are hungry, it's just assumed that this is the right thing to do. Anthropologist Sarah Blaffer Hrdy hypothesizes that this must have been the norm in prehistoric hunter-gatherer societies, "among foragers where women cooperated to keep each other's babies from fretting." Hrdy tells of ethnographic studies of cultures in central Africa and Southeast Asia where such sharing has operated as "a mutually beneficial courtesy extended by coresident women—affines, neighbors, and blood kin."

Grimm's fairy tales don't usually depict this kind of generosity. Instead, when famine looms, witches or ogres are lurking nearby, ready to pounce. Not too far distant is the American culture of divorce, which seems generally to assume that each party will struggle fiercely to guard its own supply of food and other resources; everyone knows of bitter divorces where couples have battled for larger shares. The law provides for "no-fault" dissolutions of marriages and marital assets, but it's the rare human being who can calmly forgo grasping and blaming, in divorce or other matters. And so the law steps in in another way, mandating the terms of custody and requiring regular payments to support children's needs. All too often, statistics show, mothers and children come up short: after divorce, men's economic situation tends to improve and women's to decline. Inadequate child support awards, poor enforcement of their fulfillment, women's lower wages, and the high costs of child care are largely to blame.

When divorced fathers remarry, their wives—now stepmothers—cannot avoid being part of this picture. Will the new wife spend all of her husband's money, draining the inheritance of his first wife's children? Will she favor her children from a previous marriage, or children later born to the new marriage, diverting the father's resources and attention away from his older children? It can happen. A recent study of how contemporary family structures complicate elder care, burial, and inheritance concluded that the process of dividing inherited wealth leads to conflict between adult children and their stepmothers in a majority of cases. And apparently, this is nothing new. The harmony of white stepfamilies in early America was often affected by conflict between stepparents' and stepchildren's economic interests, historian Lisa Wilson concluded after reviewing countless court records, diaries, and letters. In a time when women had few economic rights, stepfathers were more likely to wrest wealth from their stepchildren than stepmothers were, but even so, children were not unreasonable to worry when their fathers remarried. Although Wilson does not report any instances of child abandonment in the wild forests of New England, she presents ample evidence that stepmothers should not always have been trusted with the keys to the larder.

Both the household of Kristen's mother and the household of her father had enough money and enough food. Arrangements for child support operated smoothly. But we human beings can be so ravenous. Even Kristen's relative good fortune did not mean that her starvation was unthinkable. Nor did it mean that none of the adults in her life wanted to eat her up, in one way or another.

While eating pancakes in our pajamas on the morning after I had mortared together the little house of sweets, Kristen and I considered which pieces of candy should go on the roof, by the door, along the foundation, and on the walls.

"The licorice belongs on the top of the roof," she declared. "Gumdrops go along the bottom of the walls." I was impressed by her confidence and aplomb as a designer. I prepared another batch of icing as she moved the candies into position.

"Okay, let's do it!" I said, squirting a sticky sweet line along the peak of the roof. "Red or black?"

"Red," she replied. She selected a piece of licorice, held it next to the rooftop, planned her move, and gently set it in place.

No sooner had she let go than the entire structure swayed. One side of the pitched roof slid slowly onto the shiny foil base. The other side followed a few seconds later. Then, one by one, the walls teetered and collapsed. Soon all that remained was a mound of gingerbread shards and several colorful piles of candy. I wanted to cry. Kristen, however, was calm and upbeat.

"It doesn't matter," she said. "I already made one of these last week at home. My mom and I make one every year."

Now I really wanted to cry. But I managed not to. Instead, I stuffed my mouth with candy. Kristen did too. It turned out not to be such a terrible morning after all, or so it seemed at the time.

A few days later, Mark received a phone call from his ex-wife. She wanted to tell him that she'd been concerned when Kristen returned home after Christmas. She seemed to have gained some weight. What were we feeding her? Whatever it was, could we please cut back? This was not just a matter of Christmas excess, Bekka added. She had noticed little ripples of fat on her daughter's body after each of Kristen's visits, year-round.

Mark and I talked for hours that night, trying to make sense of Bekka's complaint. To our eyes, Kristen didn't seem overweight at all; she was slender, in a healthy ten-year-old girl kind of way. Perhaps our standards simply differed; after all, Bekka was a little thinner than Kristen, while I was a bit thicker. I surely served, and ate, dessert more often than Bekka did. At the same time, I believed (and still believe) that our diet, taken as a whole, was balanced, nourishing, and well-suited to a growing child. Bekka's question— "What are you feeding her?"—felt like an insult to both my body and my capacity as a caregiver. It also felt, to me, like an intrusion into one of my favorite aspects of the domestic life Mark and I shared with each other and, as often as possible, with Kristen. For his part, Mark focused immediately on a different set of issues. What might Bekka's concerns about weight mean for Kristen as she matured? Would his daughter be adequately nourished? Was she destined to be not just slender but skinny, starting down a path that can lead to illness in adolescent girls?

Mark decided to talk this over with Tom, a wise friend of ours who happened to be a psychotherapist. Tom advised Mark not to make an issue of Kristen's weight. The worst outcome in this situation, Tom said, would be for her eating to become an emotional battleground. If Kristen came to regard food as a point of conflict between her mother and her father, her health would be at far greater risk than if we quietly deferred to Bekka's concerns. Perhaps portions would be smaller in Minnesota than in Indiana, and perhaps we would need to cut back on desserts. Accepting these realities would require small changes in Mark's and my attitudes and behavior, but they would guard Kristen against an internal conflict that could be disastrous. This advice made sense to both Mark and me.

Almost thirty years later, Bekka is thin, and I am a shade plumper than just right. Kristen is slender and healthy, and so are her two children.

Hansel and Gretel turn out to be the heroes of their fairy tale. The witch imprisons Hansel in a shed, aiming to fatten him up in preparation for her feast. Each day she comes to pinch his finger to see if he is getting plump—witches have poor eyesight, the Grimms remind their readers—and each day he holds out a chicken bone instead. Finally, the witch grows impatient and decides to cook and eat both children. She instructs Gretel, whom she has forced into ceaseless domestic labor, to prepare the oven. Gretel, a clever girl, asks the witch to show her how—and then shoves the witch into the flames and slams shut the door. Gretel releases her brother from captivity, and the two fill their pockets with the witch's jewels and head home to reunite with their now wid-owed father.

When I look back across the years on my relationship with my stepdaughter, my own actions stand out in my mind. I can become so smug I'm obnoxious: how valiant, selfless, and creative I was! I baked gingerbread, and even though I could not build a little house of sweets, at least I tried—and I did prepare a nice life-sized room for her. I read stories, I purchased gifts, and I served tasty meals. Some-times my efforts seemed to succeed, and sometimes they collapsed right in front of me.

In retrospect, though, I can see that the relationship we came to have was also—perhaps especially—her doing. She could have pushed me into the oven, but instead, she sat with me for hours nibbling gumdrops and humoring my sugarplum visions. I believe that her fondest desire and deepest need was to reunite with her father, which she by and large attained. I also believe that she was usually glad I was there when she arrived to see him.

I have a friend—a woman who is far from witchy—whose preteen stepchildren did, in effect, push her into the oven. Life with them was a nightmare, she recalls. Never mind cute little houses decorated with candy; for her, the question was whether the large brick house she shared with these chil-dren and their father would stand. This family came through those difficult initial years intact, and things are much better now, but that is not always the outcome. Researchers report that stepfamilies break up at least as often as first-marriage families do. Interestingly, discord between spouses about how to deal with children is a major source of marital trouble in families of both kinds. And in stepfamilies, many studies have shown, the stress arising from this and other conflicts falls much more heavily on stepmothers than on mothers, fathers, or stepfathers.

Regardless of the legal or biological means by which children have entered our lives, those of us who care for children have tremendous power over them, power that is awful in every sense. We really can lock them up, or feed them too much or too little, or absorb their energies in ways that serve our needs, not theirs. We can also be trustworthy and caring. And yet children are not only the recipients of what adults do. Though we can try our damnedest to lure them inside, we cannot control their responses. They have power too, though of a different kind and degree. They can hurt us; they can reward us; they can dish out a heap of appalling actions and emotions; they can light up our lives. Like us, they are complicated human beings—created in God's image, endowed with reason and moral sense, and already active as unique characters in the still-unfolding family stories we share.

As I look back on those winter days of gingery construction, I'm overwhelmed with gratitude that Kristen hung in there with me, smiling and licking her fingers even as my fantasy house collapsed in ruins. What felt like failure, then, becomes a moment of special sweetness, now. Marrying a child's parent doesn't get you a relationship with that child; it doesn't bestow any rights—legal, cultural, or emotional. It just gets you in the room with her. Then it's up to both of you to find a way forward together. As another stepmother has said, "I was at the mercy of my stepchildren's avowal of my identity. I was a stepmother because my stepchildren allowed it to be."

Whatever relationship there is emerges along a two-way path that runs through deep woods, where desire and fear sometimes leap out to startle you. I confess I have a bit of the witch in me; I have tried to lure Kristen in with sweets of one kind or another on more than this occasion, for the sake of my own needs and ambitions as much as for her sake. I can see that in myself, and it's good to acknowledge it even if I also think I see in others a similar hunger to eat her up. And I also have a bit of lost child in me. It's so easy for a comment from Bekka to throw me into uncertainty, stirring up questions about how secure the grip of Kristen's hand in mine really is.

7

SCARCITY

My experience as a stepmother has been shaped by the assumption that one child cannot have two mothers. Create competition for a role as intimate and powerful as motherhood and someone might die.

There's a two-mother story in the Hebrew Bible where two women have each given birth to a son. After one of the babies dies, one woman charges the other with secretly switching the dead baby's body for the living child. The case is brought before King Solomon. There are no witnesses, just two distraught women, each bereaved in her own way. The king's adjudication of the case has long been touted as evidence of his wisdom. "Divide the living boy in two," he orders, demanding a sword. "Then give half to the one, and half to the other." Expressing compassion, and displaying far more wisdom than Solomon has shown with his risky manipulation, the woman whose baby is still alive cries out: "Please, my lord, give her the living boy; certainly do not kill him!" The second woman, on the other hand, is willing to allow the child's death rather than lose custody.

Although there are no stepmothers in this story and no swords in mine, I'm haunted by the competitive struggle it depicts. The one at greatest risk is the child. The one who sets things right and emerges with the child in her arms is his biological mother. This story depicts an order embedded deep in our culture.

I don't want to overturn this order altogether. I just want people to notice its sway and to begin to envision alternative narratives. Alternatives like, "I know I'm not this child's mother, but the care I give this child is motherly. The love from which it flows is real love, and my involvement can be good for us all."

When I venture onto Facebook pages for stepmothers, I see countless comments that explode with resentment. Many of the stepmothers who post are furious that their stepchildren are so devoted to their mothers and so oblivious to their mothers' flaws. These mothers, of course, are almost always judged undeserving of the extra portion of love they apparently receive. They have refused to follow the agreed-upon visitation schedule! They have spoiled the kids rotten! They have insulted the stepmother in the presence of the child!

Some mothers do find ways to disrupt shared custody or create emotional discord, though I doubt that all the mothers described in these posts are as wicked as their accusers assert. At the same time, I have no doubt of the emotional power behind the stepmothers' accusations. In the motherhood hierarchy of contemporary America, the mother reigns supreme, while the stepmother receives little recognition and considerable hostility. No wonder some take to online groups to vent and to seek affirmation and advice from their peers.

Some stepmothers also disrupt custody plans and sow emotional discord, to be sure; trouble can run in either direction or both. No matter the instigator, clinical experts advise that the child's parent—that is, the stepmother's spouse, not the stepmother herself—should take the lead in negotiating a resolution. I agree. But in my experience, efforts beyond these may also be needed. Even when it's unwise to engage in conflicts with an ex, a stepmother needs to deal with conflicting feelings when they arise in her own heart.

The most helpful clinical article about stepmothering I've read is "On Becoming a Good Enough Stepmother" by

Patricia Hart, a therapist and researcher who has worked with divorced and remarried families for more than three decades. Hart has listened carefully to stepmothers, who she believes occupy the most challenging stepfamily role, especially when a biological mother is still an active parent. A stepmother often confronts intense and primitive emotions from stepchildren, their mother, and her own children. Within this emotional maelstrom, she and her spouse may also desire and expect that she'll form a loving, parent-like relationship with her stepchildren. This cluster of interpersonal challenges, combined with her own frustrated expectations, can give rise to powerful *inner* conflicts. Sometimes talking with a therapist helps a stepmother work through such conflicts, and Hart's article is addressed to people in this profession. I commend counseling to those who need or desire further help. Even outside that context, however, Hart's description of a "good enough stepmother" speaks to me.

At the core of Hart's portrait is what she calls an "internal parenting stance." This stance is similar to the internal parenting stance good enough mothers attain, though it must operate in a much more fraught and complicated context. A good enough mother, in psychological theory, is attuned to her child's needs and development so well that she can adapt appropriately as the child grows and the context changes. Knowing when to provide protection and when to allow for growing independence—when to shelter and when to back off—she is able to create a good environment for her child's development. This maternal stance combines a deep and loving investment in the child with a willingness to step back to give the child space to grow and change.

A good enough stepmother, as Hart sees it, also develops a loving parental attachment to the child. However, the stepping back she learns to do is much trickier. Like any good enough parent, she makes room for the child's growth. However, she also learns to make room for the primacy of the child's biological parents. It's complicated—but she understands that it's complicated for the child as well. As the stepmother's understanding and empathy for the child grow, she develops a more generous perspective. Drawing on her understanding and empathy, she even develops the capacity to rise above the hurt she feels when a child makes what Hart calls "rejecting or dismissing responses."

It makes sense. But where are stepmothers supposed to find the strength and equanimity necessary to be so compassionate and aware? Deliberate, rational attention to a child's perspective is indispensable, and so is serious reflection on one's own desires and vulnerabilities. But difficult feelings are also involved. A child's "rejecting and dismissing responses" can hurt long after you understand why the child made them and why they trouble you so.

In the end, this process is going to take some love—from stepmothers and also from others. (Here I start to interweave my own language with Hart's clinical perspective.)

The love we need springs from varied sources. For many, the capacity to be compassionate and understanding flows from love experienced in their own childhood. If you've been lucky, your own good enough parents or stepparents will once have shown resilient, nurturing love to you, laying the foundation for your later attachments to others, including stepchildren. (Some of us had parents who were *not* good enough, however; as a therapist, Hart often works with struggling stepmothers to heal wounds from their own childhood, increasing their capacity to love in the present.) Add to this wellspring the stepmother's love for her spouse and the spouse's love for her. Desire to support her partner's parenting and commitment to forging a good and lasting marriage encourage her when stepmothering gets hard. Her partner's love and support also provide a foundation on which she can rest in difficult times. And finally, the stepmother's love for the child and her desire to be a parent add an important kind of love to this complicated mix.

Drawing from these deep wells of love, a stepmother may develop a strong parental attachment to her step-child. Ironically, the second emotional move she'll need to make—respecting the primacy of the biological parents—can flow from the same sources. The good-enough step-mother is a loving parental presence who invests herself in the child, but she also knows, and lovingly observes, when to step back. Hart puts it bluntly: successful stepmothers learn to live with their status as "second-tier mothers."

"Second-tier" sounds harsh when used in a matter so personal and dear. And maybe it doesn't even apply to some stepmothers. For most of us who have stepped into the role after a child's parents have broken up, however, a second-tier mother is exactly what we are. And to me, it seems wise to try to figure out how to live in this potentially painful location in a way that heals and unites.

Being a second-tier mother is okay, I've decided. But it's only okay because I know I'm not a second-tier wife or a second-tier human being and because my stepdaughter knows she's not her father's second-tier child.

In the neighborhood where Mark and I lived in the early years of our marriage, most of the women were stay-at-home moms several years younger than I was. One summer day, I was standing on the sidewalk with six-year-old

Kristen, hoping to recruit some playmates for her by chatting up several women whose kids were playing nearby. In this setting, in front of this audience, Kristen piped up with what she called "a great idea."

"I know, Dorothy! You and Daddy could get a divorce, and Mommy and Stephen could get a divorce, and you could marry Stephen, and Mommy and Daddy could get married, and I could live with them and come visit you and Stephen one weekend a month!"

Rarely have I felt so embarrassed and isolated. The women around me, I assumed, would rather not acknowledge the fact that the fathers of young children sometimes get divorced and remarried; Kristen's comment was unlikely to make them regard me and Kristen as potential friends. Yet what I felt even more strongly was hurt and shame at Kristen's bold declaration of desire for her parents' reunion. Her startling act of truth-telling cast light on the jagged territory Mark's and my household occupied. It unveiled for all to see a reality I'd rather ignore.

Fortunately, I also noticed something else. Even when she imagined having her dream of living with her own two parents fulfilled, Kristen still had space in her imagination for me. She hated her parents' divorce, but she did not hate me. She liked me, and she wanted me to be in her life—in it, in fact, about as often as I actually was. Her comment showed that she liked her stepfather, Stephen, too, which was a good thing for us all.

Kristen's "great idea" did not in any way reflect my highest hopes. Her desired arrangement was not at all what I longed for. But I still saw something valuable in her imagined reconfiguration of our lives. Buried somewhere in her embarrassing comment, I felt, was at least a portion of love for me. Also present was love for her parents and her other stepparent. She even seemed to accept the prospect of traveling back and forth for the sake of love. It was messy, but it was love. Lots of love. Enough to go around.

It's one of the hardest questions many of us ask. *Is there enough love to go around?* How deep and full is the well of love on which my family depends? Is there enough love for me to get all I desire and need?

I ask this question in my own hard moments, and I also sense its power for other stepmothers I know. One, whom I mentioned earlier, cried all night after her seven-year-old stepson asked her to help him buy a Mother's Day card for his "real" mother. When she told me how hurt she had felt, I understood and commiserated. When a child expresses love for his mother, a stepmother can feel the way a child feels when he senses that his parents love a sibling more than him. But I also noticed something else. The little boy's request showed that he trusted his stepmother and knew he could count on her for help in a task he was unable to complete on his own. It's true that the request reminded her that this child loves his mother, which stung. But don't we all, stepmothers too, hope that every child will love their mother? This child's "real" mother, whether a good parent or a deficient one, will be his mother all his life long, and he will be a healthier person if he can love her with his whole heart.

A stepmother, her partner, the partner's child, the child's mother: these four are profoundly entangled in one another's lives. But what are the terms and limits of their entanglement? Does their relational system necessarily operate as a zero-sum economy? If someone gets more, does someone else get less? Is the forbearance, the mutual understanding, the regard and respect—the love—that circulate among these four limited in quantity? Is there some set amount that must be divided, like a pie? Or is there a way for the amount available to increase?

This stepmother's generosity in giving the child the help he requests just might end up adding a little love to the entire system. Providing this help would require a degree of unearned and not-strictly-required regard for the good of another (possibly difficult) person, to be sure. My friend would have to smile and chat in front of a rack of stupid cards even though she aches inside. She would have to try to please someone—the mother—who may never show similar concern for her. She would have to go beyond what many people would think is required of her.

It would not be easy. But if she could find the courage and humility to do these things, she would be acting with grace.

Grace is an effusion of generosity, a movement away from blaming the other and defending the self, even when blame and self-defense are justified. When grace happens, a lop-sided portion of extra love is added to a relationship or situation. Such grace might someday be reflected back on the giver by its recipient—but then again, it might not be. Maybe a stepmother acts with what I'm calling grace in this situation, and her generosity goes unnoticed. Maybe it even leads to new grief, since it's just possible that the mother would be livid about receiving a card selected with the help of her ex's new partner. Acting graciously is a risky business.

The notion that following rules is the path to becoming a successful stepmother dominates many current books about stepfamilies. Often the rules such books offer are quite sensible and are set forth in a helpful, encouraging way; these rules and the books that contain them are useful to many readers. A good example is *Ex-Etiquette for Parents: Good Behavior after a Divorce or Separation*, by Jann Blackstone-Ford and Sharyl Jupe. The fact that the coauthors are the current and past wives of the same man, who had children with the one he married first—in other words, these two are stepmother and mother—suggests that they have found a winning formula, and the ten rules they set forth make sense.

To me, however, rules as such provide only a first step, for efforts to be on our "good behavior" often lead into deep waters. The yearning of a stepmother in the Mother's Day card situation can't be overcome simply by learning a rule, tightening her lips, furrowing her brow, and taking pains to behave herself. In the end, the capacity to behave generously in a painful situation is a profoundly personal and spiritual matter. Each of us buckles down and follows the rules once in a while, to be sure. But when it comes right down to it, *should* is not a liberating or empowering word for either stepmother or stepchild.

The word we need even more is *grace*. Because grace disrupts the game of tit for tat and doesn't reward extra points for extra work, it's always a mystery, sneaking up to catch me by surprise. I'm loved in spite of my many flaws? Grace. I'm receiving a gift even though I didn't earn it? Grace. You're forgiving me for that slight? Grace. It's mysterious, but I see it all around, showing up in the beauty of nature and the love of other people. In the spiritual community where I make my home, we try to show grace to one another—and we also celebrate the unlimited grace that supports and sustains all creation, the grace we believe comes from God. The wellspring of God's grace is what feeds the well of compassion and understanding on which I sometimes, amazingly, draw as I relate to my stepchild, her parents, and everyone else (and they to me). God's grace is not available because I'm anywhere near perfect. It's available because God is love, infusing the universe with healing and hope.

Generosity is an expression of grace. And so is hope. Aware of grace, I can confess my mistakes and brokenness, trusting that restoration is still possible. Just as important—especially in my life as a stepmother—is this: Being aware of grace gives me courage to risk noticing whatever signs of new life are starting to break in. Grace disrupts the zero-sum economy of insecurity and resentment. Grace overwhelms scarcity. I'm grateful to be loved, and when I remember this, I become a bit more generous—never perfectly but in ways that might be helpful to myself and others. My confidence in this kind of grace is one reason I was intentional earlier in this book in speaking honestly about the losses suffered by those who have divorced or experienced their parents' divorce—and one reason we are heading toward a chapter called "Mercy." For me, these are the rhythms of grace.

Other people find somewhat different paths to a similar kind of step-generosity. Stepdad Jim Sollisch, for instance, wrote an insightful essay about his and his wife's custody of both his children and hers from previous marriages. The third of his four rules for stepparenting is this: "Just say 'Yes.'" When the kids or ex-spouses make special requests that mess with your schedule, be flexible, he urges. "Say yes. You messed with their lives. You're the reason they have a schedule. Be flexible. Say *yes* with a smile, not a caveat." In those words, I hear grace. Generosity. A touch of confession. A letting-go of rules when possible. Trust in new life.

It's easy to think of situations where prudent stepparents would be unable to say *yes*, due to concern for the child's safety or well-being. And boundaries are necessary for the full development of the new family to which a stepmother belongs. But when the unavoidable and nonlethal hurts of stepmothering intrude—"Will you help me buy a card for my 'real' mother?" or "You're not my mother!" or other hurtful remarks from both children and adults—and we step back, loosen up, and try to add love to the system with whatever acts of generosity we can manage, that's grace. Embraced, this surprising *yes*, this not-strictly-required generosity, may grow—received as a gift, shared with others, and returned to whenever we can.

8
JEALOUSY

It's a quarter to one, and the party is over. After cleaning up and saying goodbye to the guests, we have escaped the hot sun and found a quiet oasis in the living room of Kristen's small house. We: Kristen and her husband, Philip; Bekka and Stephen; Mark and I; and Phoebe, Kristen and Philip's daughter, who turns five today. Her little brother, Lucas, is upstairs napping. Kristen sets out a plate of cheese and crackers and sliced apples—lunch for the adults, and for Phoebe, Kristen hopes, an inducement to calm down after an exciting morning of birthday cake and games. But Phoebe is already settling down. Exhausted, she climbs into my lap and absently pages through one of her new books. I feel her back relaxing against my belly. Her breathing lengthens, the book drops to the floor, and her head lolls against my chest. I settle deeper into the couch and stop resisting the downward tug of my own eyelids.

Suddenly both Phoebe and I are jolted awake. Bekka stands above us. Without speaking, she scoops Phoebe out of my arms. Bearing the sleepy child, she finds an armchair and relaxes into its soft embrace. My arms are empty, my lap is cold. I am bereft. Confused. Furious.

I have to admit that I don't really know what was in Bekka's mind at that moment. I do know what I was thinking and what I still believe to be true: *Bekka cannot bear to see me and Phoebe together like this.*

In that crowded room, on that September afternoon, I said nothing. Once Mark and I were alone in the car, the tears and anger I'd been holding back erupted. "Oh my God, can you believe what she did?" I cried. But Mark had not noticed Bekka's grab for his granddaughter.

"I'm so sad you feel this way," he crooned in a condescending tone of voice I had heard him use on fussy children. He was trying to comfort me, I guess, but he was actually making things worse by failing to acknowledge what had happened. He even seemed to think that a few minutes of wimpy comfort-talk were enough; a baseball game on the radio apparently interested him more. I was stunned. In the absence of his sympathy, my fuming turned inward, and my feelings of rejection and rage grew even stronger.

A few weeks later, at what seemed like a relevant point in a conversation with Kristen, I described that moment of theft again. "Oh, really?" she said. "I didn't notice. How odd." Then she looked away and changed the subject. I started to wonder, Was the blindness Kristen and Mark shared an inherited trait or a deliberate conspiracy? Were they willing to ignore such an event in order to keep the peace? Was I being too sensitive? Or were the two of them so securely situated in that sleepy little circle of soft couches that they simply did not notice when a peripheral member of the group was shoved to the side?

Mark's and Kristen's responses confirmed a thought that had crossed my mind in that moment and grown in the months that followed: the periphery of that circle is exactly where I belong. Bekka is a very engaged grandmother to Phoebe; she lives nearby and cares for Kristen's children often and well. Bekka has made far more space for them in her home and life than I have in mine, just as she has always made more space for Kristen. She was even the one who had brought the birthday cake and served it proudly to Phoebe's friends. Mark and I live almost five hundred miles away and see Phoebe and Lucas only four or five times a year. I love them tremendously, but I could hardly claim the close-ness that Bekka has offered and earned.

I wasn't surprised when I later read a study reporting that stepmothers often feel pushed aside. Canadian psychologist Elizabeth Church heard this feeling repeatedly described in her interviews with over a hundred predominantly white, middle-class stepmothers. Jealousy is an emotion many know well. But as unpleasant as it is to be jealous, what's worse is the emotion that often follows it: shame. The stepmothers in Church's study feel really, really bad about feeling jealous. A fairy tale pattern is reversed. In "Snow White," a stepmother expresses her jealousy by feeding a poisoned apple to her rival. In real life, stepmothers eat the poisoned apple themselves while trying to repress feelings others might deem wicked.

It's true: I'm uneasy about feeling jealous, and I'm reluc-tant to express the rage my jealousy arouses. Look at how quick I have been to defend Bekka! Even when burning with anger, I find myself taking pains to portray her as the one who has the greater right to cuddles, to time, even to love. What I say of her is true—but why am I so quick to say it, when friends to whom I tell the Phoebe-grab story are typically outraged by Bekka's move? Elizabeth Church's analysis would suggest that my primary motive is to make sure no one thinks I'm getting greedy or failing to appreciate

Bekka's faithful care of Kristen and her children. Seeming to defend Bekka, I am actually defending myself from a culture-driven assumption that has wormed its way into my self-understanding. I'm the stepmother, after all, and you know how wicked they are.

But couldn't I just have held that sleeping child on my lap a little longer? Was it wicked to desire that simple pleasure?

Jealousy can be an explosive force in stepfamilies. There are so many triangles in play, so many opportunities for one person to feel excluded when she sees two others feeling close. Occasionally a triangle turns deadly. In *Phaedre*, a classic French drama based on a Greek myth, a stepmother lusts after her husband's son; when the curtain falls, both stepson and stepmother are dead. More often, at least in my relatively calm and secure corner of the world, the emotional imbalance is less lethal, but someone is hurt or excluded even so. Here are a parent and a child—and a third party, a stepparent. A child's two parents—and a third party, a stepparent. A parent and a new spouse—and a third party, a child. A parent and a child—and a third party, a parent who is also a former spouse. A new spouse and a child—and a parent who is also a former spouse. Fill in different genders, multiply for additional children and spouses, and the possibilities for exclusion and jealousy are endless.

For stepmothers, this often means feeling shut out by the preexisting bonds between their partners and their stepkids. I know of a child who always found a way to sidle between her father and his new wife at the sink or on the couch. But this is not the only triangle that can cause pain. Feelings of being the Insider or the Outsider—pick your triangle—are signals of what psychologist and therapist Patricia Paper-now calls "the first challenge" of stepfamily life. This first challenge is to keep the pain-inducing triangles that are unavoidably present at the beginning from hardening into enduring patterns.

On that September afternoon, I began by presuming that Bekka was jealous of me. Before long, I was stewing in jealousy of my own. If my hunch about Bekka's feelings is accurate, there was more than enough jealousy to go around that day, even though in that situation we were grandmothers, not mothers. You'd think our aging would have eased the tension—though actually, I've noticed, few grandparents are eager to share with others the time and hugs of their grandchildren. I feel the same possessiveness toward my birth daughter's daughter as Bekka was displaying toward Phoebe. Further, thirty years of feelings about Kristen, framed by Bekka's primacy and my own questions about where I fit, must have been resonating in the warm air of that small house. Triangles don't necessarily collapse even when a generation's time has passed.

Though it's hard to remember this when you're feeling jealous, jealousy is an emotion that often runs in both directions. Three parties are involved, and the role of odd person out gets passed back and forth. Brooklyn writer and comedienne Laura Lifshitz published a moving essay that gives a divorced mother's point of view on this dynamic. Her four-year-old daughter has just spent the weekend with her father and his girlfriend for the first time. "What did you do?" Laura asks the child upon her return. "We snuggled and watched the Disney short fil-ums," she happily replies. Laura trembles with possessive rage, remembering the difficult pregnancy by which she gained this child and constructing imaginary scenes of losing her. "I wished every evil upon this person with a vengeance I have never felt before," she confesses. She burns with jealousy, but "not because of my former husband. It's about my daughter."

I have been divorced, and on the basis of that experience, I believe Lifshitz when she says that she is over her former husband and ready for him to be with someone else. And I am a mother as well as a stepmother; because of that experience, I believe that the rage she feels really is about her daughter. When I imagine my own child snuggling for a weekend with another woman, I can hardly bear it. This is not a snuggle with an aunt or a sitter. This is a snuggle set within a potential new home that is configured in a way that looks an awful lot like the home from which the child originally came. Father. Mother. Child. Only it's not my home, and I'm not the mother in that scene.

Lifshitz is a good mother. She faces her insecurities and masters her rage, at least in the moment that matters. As she listens to the child's report on the weekend, she gushes over details and does everything she can to assure her daughter that it's okay that she enjoyed being with Daddy and his friend. Two weeks later, she even writes a letter to this woman, thanking her for the hospitality she showed the little girl. The letter seems to me a little over the edge, a way of saying "she's mine, back off" while ostensibly making nice. Still, this mother's effort to be as accepting as possible—and especially her resolve not to poison the mind of the child—is admirable. If the relationship between the father and his girlfriend endures, countless opportunities for hurt will arise as the child moves back and forth between two households, raising practical and emotional issues as yet unimagined.

Laying a foundation of goodwill at the beginning will have served everyone well. But this does ask a lot of everyone concerned, perhaps especially the mother. Over time, divorced mothers like Lifshitz will have to deal not with one weekend of snuggling but with many childless Christmases and New Year's Eves. They will have to step aside repeatedly over the years as their children develop family memories to which they, the mothers, will have no access.

The relationship between a mother and a stepmother is crucial. There we suffer, both of us, at least from time to time. And there we do something extremely important: we rise above ourselves for the sake of a child. Bekka and I never talked about this directly; each of us just forged ahead as bravely as she could, or so it seems to me. The main source of the balance I've been able to maintain amid all the emotional triangles we were navigating has been gratitude to Bekka for supporting Kristen's relationship with me. So I'd say this to Lifshitz: good job! And this to her daughter's eventual stepmother: notice and appreciate the mother's good job!

The Phoebe-grab put me back on the cross for a moment. But when I remember Bekka's prior generosity, my resentment dies once again. This does not mean I have forgotten the grab; obviously, I have not. But it does mean that each time I see Bekka, I try to be a little more generous in return. It's just that, on occasion, I have to swallow hard and think about it before I speak.

* * *

I experienced this need for slow and careful speech last autumn, as emails circulated about Thanksgiving plans. As usual, dinner would be at son John's and dessert at daughter Martha's, with Kristen bringing hors d'oeuvres and a pie. In the past, Kristen and her husband and kids have typically spent the day after Thanksgiving at Bekka's—but this year Martha had an idea that might upset that pattern. She sent a group invitation: Did anyone want to go to the *Sing-Along Sound of Music* at a downtown theatre on that Friday? Martha's five-year-old, Naomi, was obsessed with this movie after watching it at home. I was overcome with matrilineal joy: my mother took me to see Mary Martin, her second cousin, portray Maria von Trapp on Broadway when I was a girl. Yes! Let's do it! Soon John signed his family up too.

Kristen's response came only to me. She had asked her mother about plans for that day, and now she had a question. She asked it tentatively, almost apologetically, assuring me that I was under no obligation. Would it be okay if her mother and aunt came as well?

"Is that too weird?" she asked. It's as if I'd have trouble being around my lover's old girlfriend. Surely Kristen knew that wouldn't bother me. I did have a problem, though. I definitely wanted Kristen and her family at the sing-along; I had great memories of watching *The Sound of Music* with

Phoebe when she was Naomi's age and similarly obsessed. But when we gather to watch this on the big screen—Mark and I and our three kids, three kids-in-law, and grandchildren—*I* wanted to be the Mother Superior. Instead, I was going to find myself in a secondary maternal position once again, at least with some of them. This has happened so many times. What caused me pain—pain, not weirdness—was that I have spent most of my life loving a child who loves me less than she loves Bekka. And that would be on display once again at the sing-along.

I knew I'd say yes, but I struggled over how to respond. Might this request provide an occasion to explain to Kristen what I find difficult in our triangulated relationships? Kristen seems to have no sense of how often I'm confronted with her persistent attentiveness to and love for her biological mother—even though she gets quite upset if I seem to focus on my biological children more than on her, which I admit I sometimes do.

A message began to form in my mind, though not on my screen: "I'd be glad for your mom and aunt to come. But don't you see that once again, I'm being shoved into secondary status with you and your kids? We all know who the real mother and grandmother is for you! You are so sensitive to anything that suggests that I give more to John and

Martha—time, presence, help—than to you. You seem to fear that they, not you, are the ones who really matter to me. Likewise, I often feel that although I am allowed into your life, it's never possible to shift your daughterly regard from Bekka to me, even for a moment. Don't you see that your availability to me is always conditional and secondary?"

Instead, I wrote, "It would be much more fun to go with a bigger group, like this would be. Go ahead and check it out with them. I hope it works. Love, Dot."

Before long, our whole group received a joyful message from Bekka, who sounded delighted and grateful to be included. Martha sent a warm and welcoming response. And I breathed a sigh of relief. I easily could have messed this up, but I didn't. Whew. The presence of Bekka and her sister wouldn't make that big a difference in the excursion, I realized—at least not as big a difference as forcing Kristen to choose between her two sets of parents would create.

As it turned out, Mark and I missed the show due to a snowstorm. Everyone else had a great time, and I felt fine about it. But this episode has continued to unsettle me. Here I am, telling about my restrained and loving response, as if I could now gain the credit I did not claim at the time. Moreover, I haven't, until now, acknowledged how considerate Kristen was when asking for my permission. This was good of her, and I am grateful.

Here's the deal, which I write here for the sake of other stepmothers who may have similar feelings. Kristen deals with triangles more often than I do, and yes, the needs and feelings of the child—even when she is an adult—have priority. Still, I wish someone would notice what this step-mother goes through as well and how much a stepmother can contribute to whatever happiness not just one but two families attain.

That's as honest as I can be.

Even as I stew over my desire for recognition and appre-ciation, which I've assumed is unrequited, I also realize that this is not the whole story. Perhaps my wishes have been granted more fully than I've ever realized. Kristen was obviously aware that it might be tough for me to share a big family event with her mother; Kristen showed lots of regard for my feelings, asking me in a loving way and thanking me as warmly and sincerely as anyone could do. As for Bekka, I could tell how pleased she was to be included, and her expressions of thanks were as sincere and plentiful as Kris-ten's. I even understand, now, that she probably felt left out at times when Kristen was with me and Mark, just as Laura Lifshitz felt after another Thanksgiving.

We never really know what's in the hearts of others. Thus the triangles that deserve our greatest attention are the ones we ourselves have erected and nurtured. This means trying to comprehend what's in our own hearts while being as generous as possible in interpreting the behavior and motives of others.

With this in mind, I decide to revisit the warm, drowsy afternoon when Phoebe turned five. I go back to the comfy chair, the little girl on my lap, the book on hers. I feel such peace and joy—leaning my cheek on her hair, cradling her body, savoring the maternal feelings coursing through my own. The situation is not so different from the one the white-haired gentleman disrupted some thirty years before. Between those two afternoons, I learned a lot about the family role I took up when I married Mark. Saying the ugly word—and thinking of myself as a stepmother—is no longer shocking, to Kristen or to me. Even so, the vulnerability I began to acknowledge on that day long ago had never completely gone away. On the one hand, Kristen and I now have a strong relationship, built by the two of us across the years. On the other hand, I now understand more fully the terms of second-tier parenthood.

It's difficult to imagine a more perfect image of the insecurity intrinsic to stepmothering: Bekka grabs Phoebe from my lap, leaving me bereft, confused, and furious. This image crystallizes one of my feelings so perfectly, in fact, that I wonder if the Phoebe-grab actually happened! Did I suddenly awaken from a dream, there in that comfy chair on that warm afternoon? Was I actually ambushed not by Bekka but by some fear of loss erupting from my own inner depths? Or perhaps Phoebe reached out to Bekka as I dozed, and Bekka simply responded. I'll never know. What I do know is that my feelings were valid, even if the image was, maybe, imaginary. I also know that I don't need to stay angry at Bekka for whatever happened, or did not happen, on that afternoon.

No matter how much equanimity I muster, the fact of my peripheral status as a stepmother remains. This doesn't trouble me as much as it once did. I've come to expect and even to understand how our particular triangles work and also to be more honest about my feelings when a difficult moment startles me. It's also helpful to discover, once in a while, that others in the family recognize the difficulties of my position and reflect on these things too. I'm finally getting better at noticing and appreciating it when they do.

A few years ago, Kristen sent me a beautiful story she had encountered on the website brevitymag.com, which publishes very short nonfiction essays. "Thank You," by Sejal Shah, tells of the author's relationship with a divorced man who is the father of a little girl. The father's apartment is littered with small pink shoes, and there is a child seat in his car; the first time he and Sejal make love, the daughter is sleeping in the bedroom next door. The father tells Sejal he loves her, but he never makes space for her to meet his daughter. Frustrated that her romantic relationship remains separate from the child and must always be squeezed into the short span between the daughter's bedtime and the father's, Sejal breaks up with him. In this story, she addresses the little girl she never got to meet, expressing her sorrow that "I will never have the chance to love you, to be your dad's annoying girlfriend or your evil stepmother or your big sister or your babysitter or your sort-of friend."

As I read this story, I was aware that the story I had lived with Kristen and her father might also have been very brief. "How sad that would be!" I wrote to Kristen in an email. "I'm grateful for this story, and I'm grateful that this story is not mine. Thank you."

Kristen replied with her own appreciation of Shah's short essay. What most grabbed her, she wrote, was "to see what it must be like to be at the fringes of that parent-child relationship initially." As she read, what came to her was "a realization that the step-mom figure would experience feelings of jealousy or 'outsider-ness,' since I always just assumed it was the child that felt pushed out of the new relationship between the adults."

I was surprised that this perceptive woman, by this time in her thirties, had noticed neither my restriction to the fringes of her life nor how that had made me feel. That stung me a little. But far more important was that she now saw this dynamic as an adult and that she cared about what it had felt like for me. Most wonderful of all, she had discovered a point of shared experience for the two of us—once both outsiders, now insiders as well.

9

MERCY

There I am, in the same mountain village where a white-haired gentleman upset me and Kristen as we drifted off to sleep on a long-ago summer afternoon. This time, decades later, I am squeezed between Mark and Phoebe on a bench inside the Village Center. It's hot. To ease the post-Vespers transition to bed, Phoebe is already dressed in her Tinkerbell nightgown, and both of us are fidgety as we wait for things to get started. Shifting my legs on the sticky black Naugahyde, I stretch my right arm out behind her along the back of the bench. My fingers graze Bekka's left shoulder. Bekka turns toward me with a smile, and I smile too. At last, the pastor stands up, turns on her microphone, and welcomes us and other newcomers. The service begins.

Just a month ago, I was writing about how Bekka grabbed the drowsy Phoebe from my lap. And now we're sharing a moment of friendship, delighting in a little girl we both love.

It's a summer evening at Holden Village, a center for theology, social justice, and simple living located in a remote alpine valley in the North Cascade Mountains. Tonight, four hundred of us are packed into a barn-like structure built in the 1930s as a gymnasium for the miners who came here to extract ore from a nearby mountain. After the mine closed and the property was deeded to a Lutheran organization, this building became a worship space, its ceiling painted with rainbow trout, trillium, and the stars that form the constellation Orion. Outdoors, those same bits of creation move and blossom and shine for real. And so do we villagers—hiking and cooking, reading and engaging in intense conversations, watching the kids and monitoring the gauges on the hydro plant beside Copper Creek.

Holden is surrounded by untamed space. Hundreds of square miles of forests, glaciers, meadows, and peaks spread out in every direction. But the village itself is compact.

In the former miners' dormitory where Mark and I are housed, the bathroom is down the hall. The next morning, I wait for whoever is hogging the shower to hurry up and dry off. When the blue plastic curtain slides open, I see that it's Bekka. We smile at each other, though a little less broadly than we did the night before.

Later that day, I mention our cozy rooming assignments to a Holden friend.

"Oh my," she says. "I get along just fine with my husband's ex, but I wouldn't want to run into her in the shower every morning."

This place, these relationships, this family—they are wonderful. They are also complicated, even after many years.

My story as a stepmother is not a story of steady progress. I didn't work everything out and then settle into an undisturbed state of calm. Both the wonderful parts and the painful parts have been present all along, with each subsiding and erupting, unevenly and unpredictably, along the way. The joy I experienced in being with Kristen on Mark's and my honeymoon has persisted and grown—sometimes in moments of special closeness, sometimes in taken-for-granted warmth. And the challenging bits have persisted too—my insecurity in relation to her mother, my jealousy, my resistance to accepting second-tier motherhood. Time has not completely healed all wounds, in me or in other members of our complicated family.

Instead, what time has provided is many opportunities to practice being a not-so-wicked stepmother. Practice does not make perfect, mind you. But practice can prepare a person to deal wisely with negative experiences and to give more space and attention to good ones. Over the years, that's the change I see in myself: a generous response comes more readily to hand, and a sense of gratitude is easier to summon. By now I usually don't even have to think about these things, though sometimes I struggle a bit. Often grace is just there, right in the middle of the ordinary routines that have taken shape during decades of practice. You share a bathroom. You plan a movie outing. You host in your home a guest from whom you once were estranged. You hold back on desserts. You read a thousand and one stories to a little girl, and years later you read them to her children.

Mark and Bekka first visited Holden with their baby daughter. After they broke up, Bekka and Kristen traveled to Holden alone. I went to Holden for the first time on Mark's and my honeymoon, and I loved it. The following summer, Bekka and Kristen went to Holden with Bekka's new husband. He loved the place too, and each family has returned almost every year since. Sometimes we merely overlapped, which could get awkward. Sometimes we actually connected.

At first, Mark's and Bekka's second families took care not to intrude on one another's time at Holden. Each gave the other a wide berth. I don't know what Bekka and Stephen were thinking about whether to allow their trips to overlap with ours, but Mark and I were concerned. What would others think when they figured out the relations among us? And what did we think? Could we manage this thing that was supposed to be so hard? But in the end, all of us really wanted to spend time at Holden, and sometimes it just wasn't possible to settle on mutually exclusive dates, so there we were, haphazardly, together in the village. Around the time Kristen turned twelve, we realized we could solve a scheduling problem by having her go to Holden with us as summer neared its end; she would return from Holden with them, arriving back in Minneapolis in time for school. It must have pleased her immensely to have both of her parents in one place, for soon a step-version of a family reunion became an annual expectation, not only for her, but also for Mark's and my twins and Bekka and Stephen's son, all born within months of one another and now fast friends.

Though we typically kept our distance in the early years (as much as one can in a densely populated village with only one place to eat), we got along okay. Actually, it seemed to be more awkward for others than it was for us. Once, when Mark and I had to cancel our trip at the last moment, Bekka and Stephen did the chores that would have been ours, simply filling without comment the gaps created by our absence. This became a topic of ironic village gossip when a man in the throes of a difficult divorce realized what they were doing.

"You've got to be kidding me! You're doing dish team for your ex?"

One by one, countless little moves nudged open a space in which something new could emerge. Our finding the courage to share this small community, now a sacred space for both families, was crucial. But the character of the village was what mattered most. Built into the rhythms of this community were practices of reconciliation and openings for grace.

Some of these rhythms beat with a regularity first limned out hundreds of years and thousands of miles away. At Vespers each evening, we prayed and sang together. On Sundays, we passed the peace and shared Communion.

On the hot night when Phoebe sat between us in her Tinkerbell nightgown, I leaned over to Bekka when we were back in our seats after going forward to receive Communion.

"Yum. The bread was that amazing sourdough we had at dinner."

"Yum," she replied with a smile. "Best bread ever."

Steady practice drew us together in good ways. And occasionally, something big happened that redrew the picture of brokenness I had carried with me out of the past.

* * *

Every August, the Perseid meteor shower rains streams of light across the skies of the northern hemisphere. Most years I forget to look or can't see anything even if I remember, as city lights dilute the darkness and render the fast-moving flashes invisible. But sometimes this natural wonder occurs while I'm at Holden. That's what happened the summer I traveled there with a group of teenagers, including my twins. Mark and Kristen, by this time in her twenties, had returned to the Midwest, but Bekka and Stephen were still around, volunteering on Holden's short-term staff.

My friend Ingrid was hosting another group at Holden during that August week. These guests were residents of Genesis House, a ministry for women who are trying to regain their independence after years of tough living on the streets of Chicago. Their life experiences were quite different from those of the youngsters in my charge.

Ingrid suggested we get our groups together. We decided to take a star hike—Holden lingo for a late-night walk beyond the village limits into star-revealing darkness. So one night after Vespers, we rounded up a stack of yard blankets and a box of flashlights and met at the edge of the village. A few other villagers joined us. One of these was Bekka.

Everyone fell into comfortable pairs and trios as we started to trudge up the steep trail leading to the top of the tailings left behind from the defunct mine, a large, level plateau where we would get an unobstructed view of the sky. A few of the youngsters sprinted, but it took half an hour for some members of our group to make the climb. Many of the Chicago women moved tentatively; the darkness, uncompromised by streetlights, was spooky, they said, and so were the noises coming from the forest. But as we moved beyond the trees onto the top of the huge barren pile of wasted rock, everyone gasped. "I haven't seen this many stars since I was a little girl in Mississippi," my companion murmured in amazement. Looking down, we saw the village a thousand feet below, a faint circle of light twinkling in the valley's vast darkness.

Moving slowly, everyone took a blanket, spread it on the ground, and lay down to gaze up into the spangled sky. Every now and then a meteor flared across the heavens, and several times we simultaneously breathed an appreciative "ahhhhhh." Mostly, though, we were silent together as we settled one by one into our own reflective solitudes.

When all were still, the voices of two women broke the silence. One voice, young and strong, bore the accents of the Pacific Northwest. The other, older, moved to rhythms rooted in the Deep South. Alternating verse by verse, these voices lifted up a psalm in the hearing of this unusual assembly of stargazers:

Praise the Lord, sun and moon; sing praise, all you shining
  stars.
Praise the Lord, heaven of heavens, and you waters above
  the heavens.
Let them praise the name of the Lord, who commanded,
  and they were created,
who made them stand fast forever and ever.

I'm not sure how long we remained under that star-streaked sky, side by side on the yard blankets. But as I lay there, I became aware of a startling paradox. I was on top of a massive, toxic scar on the face of the earth. And I was also surrounded by beauty beyond human imagining. A few decades before, human beings had wrecked the land beneath us; they had made money, and I had benefited too as a place of retreat became available to me. But the earth had paid the price. Fish could no longer survive in the river below, and deer could not drink from it. Even so, it seemed to me, as clear as the stars themselves, that God still loved this land and these creatures, including us, including me. With the psalmist, I rejoiced: "Praise the Lord from the heavens, praise God in the heights!" Blessed be this strong darkness, these streaming lights, this silence. Blessed be God's creative power and God's promise to make all things new.

Finally, an impulse to share my awe led me to sit up and look around. What I saw overwhelmed me in a different way. My daughter Martha was lying nearby, serenely sharing her yard blanket with two women. On her right was a woman who was striving to overcome immense hardship in a city near our home. On her left was Bekka, the mother of her sister, the first wife of her dad.

So much brokenness was gathered right in front of me—the failed marriage, the difficult stepfamily, the suffering long borne by a resolute woman whose name I did not know. And on the same blanket was this girl of my own flesh, so young, so delighted by this midnight excursion, so deeply woven into my own hopes and joys and fears—and, undeniably, so vulnerable to the same kinds of brokenness the women on both sides of her had already experienced. It was overwhelming. But I could also see, in the very same glance, that all the brokenness gathered there was being overcome in that moment, as these three shared an old blanket, heard some ancient words, and witnessed a display of cosmic beauty.

That night has stayed with me as a foretaste of the healing of the world—the healing of creation, the healing of divisions of race and class, and the healing of broken families and persons. For me, this was a glimpse of the really real, a shimmering moment when the reconciliation I believe God intends for all became visible.

We human beings tend to break things. Hearts. Covenants. Ecosystems. A marriage may be among the least of what we break. When I remember lying atop a toxic waste site and praying under the stars with women brutalized by injustice, I feel like the ruptures experienced by a middle-class family amount to little more than a hill of beans.

As I've been writing this book, some readers have asked, "What's the big deal?" Why do I insist on pondering the strains within my unexpected, reconfigured family, which, after all, is a pretty good family as families go? We don't see a problem, these readers say; people today are unlikely to judge any person, or any family form, as if only one pattern were the norm. Some of these comments come from friends who know Kristen. She seems to be doing just fine, and they've seen the two of us together and that seems fine too, as indeed it is. When they look at Mark's and my marriage, they don't see anything that's particularly different from their own first-marriage unions. They know John and Martha, and they have seen these two with Kristen, and they think of the three of them as full-fledged siblings and deep friends, as these three also think of themselves. So what's the big deal? So many people get divorced these days or separate without ever marrying in the first place. Single parents and stepparents are everywhere. Less than half of American kids live with their two original parents. Why am I upset? Am I imagining, or displaying, an outmoded form of judginess?

I'm simply trying to say it matters. When we break the covenants that underlie our primary relationships, it matters. Wounds are opened, and infections set in: lack of trust, simmering resentment, poor-me, horrible-you. Material resources get reallocated, fairly or not. Loyalties must be renegotiated. Thanks be for the right to divorce, when justly enforced. And yet. That is not the end of it. Something broken remains.

I'm also saying that it matters that there is, loose in the world, a mercy that can make all things new, even in our fragile and fallible families. Life and hope are not restored when someone says, "It doesn't matter." Life and hope are restored when someone says, "Go in peace, you are forgiven."

This is where it begins. A situation is broken, and so are the people who inhabit it. Everybody involved has flaws—but that observation is so obvious it's banal. Saying "nobody's perfect" doesn't get us very far. People are not only imperfect, they're imperfect in relation to specific other people. They have hurt one another. They have let one another down. They have puffed themselves up while belittling others. It sounds like a stepfamily, and perhaps it is. But it could also be a workplace, where someone gets promoted unfairly while someone more deserving loses out. It could be a religious community, where an old fight over money still burns holes in one person's heart and another person's wallet. It could be a classroom, where the student with the highest grade has secretly been cheating.

And this is what comes next, in any of these situations. We are honest about where we've gone wrong—that is, we confess our own failures. And we listen for similar expressions of sorrow or regret from others, trying not to shut them out so completely that we can't hear whatever honesty they may be offering. Whether they do any confessing or not, we don't pretend that we are without fault. Then we turn, humbly and hopefully, toward the promise of new life.

When we listen carefully, it's just possible that we'll detect small notes of love breaking through the ambient noise of our messy relationships. These notes are worth noticing. We might, for example, realize that a stepchild's request to help him do something loving for his mother is a sign that things are moving in the right direction. We might share a bathroom with a smile, remembering the communion into which we entered the previous night. We might take time, once in a while, to rest beneath the stars and soak up the love and presence of the God who made the stars and who made us, even if our resting place is a pile of toxic rubble. And these small portions of love, these pinpricks of light, sometimes expand. Light has a way of transforming darkness, once you let it in.

Even to imagine "mercy" is to open yourself to the possibility that more love is available to you, and to others, than you once suspected. When I was a divorced woman, alone in Chicago, Mark's desire to cherish me and invite me into his life felt like mercy. I had known rejection and doubted my worth, but now love overwhelmed loss, and acceptance overwhelmed imperfection. In the decades since, I haven't always been easy to live with, and neither has he. Yet what we've most needed has often welled up within and between us—a flowing spring of unearned love, a sense of encompassing grace. This mercy is beyond what we can muster on our own. We believe it comes from God. Trusting that God is merciful, we reaffirm, again and again, that love really is stronger than hate. Love is also stronger than social custom and propriety, including prejudices about what form our family or other families should take. This kind of love is even stronger than the awful little things that annoy us about one another.

I want to share some of the way of thinking and living that provides the source and motive of my trust in God's love and mercy. In my experience, this is the most reliable source of the grace I've needed as a stepmother, though I realize that other people find what they need in other places. Some readers are already more attuned to this way of thinking and living than I am, while it will be relatively unfamiliar to others. To some readers, I suspect, it will seem misguided, or worse—perhaps because certain people who claim to speak for the very tradition to which I belong interpret this tradition quite differently. "Christian"—a name I gladly wear—has been weaponized by some of the people who also claim it, and hurtful approaches to family and sexuality are prominent in their arsenal. For those of us whose experience has disrupted the Dad-and-Mom-and-Dick-and-Jane model of family, there are strong reasons to be suspicious of Christianity. But there are also powerful reasons to draw on this faith tradition as we seek to form families shaped by mercy and love.

Among these is the description of love often read at weddings:

If I speak in the tongues of mortals and of angels, but do not have love, I am a noisy gong or a clanging cymbal. And if I have prophetic powers, and understand all mysteries and all knowledge, and if I have all faith, so as to remove mountains, but do not have love, I am nothing. If I give away all my possessions, and if I hand over my body so that I may boast, but do not have love, I gain nothing.

Love is patient; love is kind; love is not envious or boastful or arrogant or rude. It does not insist on its own way; it is not irritable or resentful; it does not rejoice in wrongdoing, but rejoices in the truth. It bears all things, believes all things, hopes all things, endures all things. Love never ends.

This passage comes from a letter written around the year 54 CE in a provincial city of the Roman Empire. Its author, Paul, was a religious leader who traveled around the Mediterranean world telling people about Jesus and organizing communities among those who responded to his message. Here Paul is writing to one of those communities—an *ecclesia*, a *koinonia*, a *church*—which he founded in the Greek city of Corinth. The community is in turmoil, he has heard. There are arguments; cliques and hierarchies have emerged; and some people think that *their* gifts, like eloquence or having lots of knowledge or contributing lots of money, are superior to the gifts of others.

Throughout the letter, Paul addresses the specific quarrels and insults that are tearing this community apart. However, an overarching theme holds the letter together: Paul's conviction that the love God has shown to the members of this community is the foundation of their life together. He writes to remind the squabbling Corinthians of what it means to be *in communion* with God and with one another. To be in communion is to embrace a state of mutuality, openness, and loving regard toward one another.

Paul's stirring account of love was written for an assembly of fractious people, not for a wedding. People who respond to Jesus's message still form communities (I belong to one), and we continue to read these words as we struggle to live together harmoniously. But we also read this part of the letter at many weddings.

Where more than in families do we need the virtues Paul names as elements of love: patience, kindness, generosity, humility, and endurance? When we hear these words applied to the future any couple will face, we realize that the love they'll need can't be fueled by romance alone. In their new family, they will need to practice love in the face of irritations and resentments. They'll be practicing love in a situation where conflicts and wrongdoing are real and where envy and arrogance often erupt. They'll need a love that flows from communion with an inexhaustible source that is larger than themselves.

Perhaps it's odd to hold up such an ideal of love in a context where love has already failed—where, for example, the parents of brides or grooms have divorced. Paul is fully aware that he's writing to people who have already failed at love. Even so, because he has confidence in the grounding reality of God's love, he believes that their communion with one another can be renewed. Indeed, the communion he envisions for them will be embodied, in part, by their membership in a new kind of family.

Writing to his far-flung gatherings of friends and followers, Paul calls them "brothers" and "sisters," and he urges them to embrace one another with this same language, regardless of biological ties. All of them, by his account, are "children of God" who have been adopted into God's family. What Paul sets forth is a family born of communion. Biological ties don't determine who's in and who's out.

Contrary to the claims of conservative twenty-first-century pundits, Jesus did not make the validation of biological families a strong emphasis in his teaching. Instead, his followers formed a new kind of family, in which some were married and some were not, some had children and some did not, all were to care for widows and orphans, and all were siblings. Yes, they argued and sometimes broke apart, but that did not necessarily spell the end of love.

Even today, people like us, stepmothers, can participate in this new kind of family, forging bonds of relationship across boundaries that once seemed insurmountable. That's what I'd call mercy.

* * *

Kristen married Philip a few months before she turned thirty. The day of the wedding was bright and clear, the setting was lovely, and everyone present seemed delighted that these two young people had found each other. As the bride's step-mother, I was in a role that's stressful for many, often because brides and their mothers resent the presence of a father's second wife. That was not a problem at this wedding. Kristen and Bekka welcomed me warmly, and the jovial head table at the reception included the bride, the groom, and all six of their parents. Though happy and glorious, however, that day was not a simple one; there was plenty of complexity to go around. This time, however, it was good complexity. As I look back, I am aware that Kristen's wedding day was one of the most important days I've had as a stepmother. As I explain why that is, please remember that what I write here represents my memories and perspective alone.

The night before the wedding, Mark and I, Bekka and Stephen, and several other guests stayed in a motel near the church. About 9 a.m. on the big day, my cell phone buzzed. It was Kristen. I was thrilled to see her name and answered eagerly, hoping for a little anticipatory chat.

"I need to talk to my mother," she stammered, choking back tears. "Her cell phone must be off. She's not answering."

"Can I help you?"

"No. Just please go find her and tell her to call me right away."

I did. Bekka took it from there. Everything turned out fine.

Talk about second-tier status. This hurt. But I'd had lots of practice. I let it go.

And off I went on my errands. Kristen had asked me to prepare the Communion for the wedding service. This meant gathering the material things needed for the ritual of Holy Communion, the meal of bread and wine that Christians share in memory of Jesus and trust in God's promise of new life. But I knew that my task included another dimension as well, for the key word here—*communion*—has two meanings in Christian theology. Holy Communion, the ritual, also provides a taste of the kind of communion Paul commended to his correspondents in Corinth—the kind of communion in which people enter into loving unity with one another, trusting that God's love will supply the needed mercy and grace. Our liturgies call this meal "a foretaste of the feast to come," because it provides a moment here on earth when we glimpse, and perhaps briefly experience, the joyful unity that God has in store for us and all creation at the end of time.

This was an assignment I relished. The church had cups and napkins for Holy Communion, but I thought they were too fancy. So I walked to a gift shop downtown and searched for worthy substitutes. None of the napkins I found were suitable, since the occasion surely demanded cloth rather than paper and white rather than orange or green. I finally settled on a cotton dishtowel, which I later cut into quarters. To hold the wine, I found two large goblets that had been turned on a potter's wheel and roughly glazed in white. They were a little heavy and not at all churchy, but they would do.

Soon it was time to meet Mark for lunch and then to return to the motel to dress for the wedding. A couple of hours before the ceremony, we headed to the church, where we delivered the goblets and napkins and reported for choir practice. The groom's father, a choral conductor by profession, had issued an invitation to wedding guests to join him in preparing a song for the service, and Mark and I, John and Martha, Kristen's stepfather, and several others had responded. Our conductor led us through the song a few times and declared us ready.

As the church began to fill with guests, the wedding party milled about in a large room in the back of the building. Kristen sent me a message to come see her in the room where she was preparing. I was overwhelmed by how beautiful she was, and how happy, and how ready for this marriage. I told her that; I said "I love you"; and a moment later, both of us were hurried along to find our spots in the processional. We processed. The whole congregation sang a hymn or two. We gazed in approval and support upon the young couple, so well suited to each other. We stood and declared together that we would support them in the years to come. We listened to a sermon that I recall was wonderful, though I've forgotten the specifics. And then the groom's father stood and beckoned the choir to gather near the piano.

Singing with the choir is what most stays with me from that day. I think that's because the song we sang is all about communion, in both senses. The words come from the Gospel according to John, written late in the first century by an unknown author who called himself "the beloved disciple." In a long discourse delivered just before his arrest and execution by the Roman authorities, Jesus tells his closest followers how he hopes they will live once he is gone. These followers are usually called disciples, but here Jesus also calls them friends. What he wants for them is communion: unity and love that are rooted in God's own love. Speaking in poetic images, he invites them to join their lives to a network of relationships infused with abundant love. "I am the vine," he tells his friends. "You are the branches."

As I sang these words, I heard Stephen's voice behind me, mingling with Mark's. I saw Kristen and Philip, hand in hand in their seats, watching and listening. Behind them was Bekka, misty-eyed. Next to me was Martha, and behind her was John, both adding their strong young voices to the song. In the company of all these beloveds, the harmony of the music gave way to harmony of a different kind, and my heart overflowed. All of us are indeed branches of God's vine, I realized. All of us are related, under the bark and down at the root, soaking up the water and breathing in the air of God's good earth. Together, we are nourished by a love beyond our making and deserving.

When the song was done, we choir members returned to our seats, and the service continued. A few minutes later, I was standing in the front again, next to Kristen, facing the congregation. Now I was not only experiencing communion; I was also, with Kristen, serving the meal of Communion to those who came forward to receive it.

She placed bread into each open hand, saying, "This is the body of Christ, given for you." And then I lifted the white-glazed goblet to each person's lips, saying, "This is the blood of Christ, shed for you."

At one point, Kristen leaned over to me and whispered, "I *love* that pottery cup!"

It was a foretaste of the feast to come.

10

VOCATION

Today is my birthday. Kristen is now older than I was when she and I first met, and her daughter, Phoebe, is older than Kristen was at that time. Phoebe is seven. I am turning sixty-eight.

Mark and I are just sitting down to supper when the shrill *brrrrr* of a FaceTime call interrupts us. Hoping it might be a birthday call from one of the kids, I rush into the kitchen, grab my phone, and figure out which button to press. Kristen appears, then Phoebe. "Happy birthday, Dot!" they exclaim together. I am delighted they remembered. There they are. Both are waving at me on the little screen, alike in sweatshirts and leggings, dark blonde hair framing their faces.

It turns out that this call, ostensibly a gift, also brings a request. "Phoebe has to interview somebody for school,"

Kristen says, "and she wants it to be you. Do you have time for that?" Absolutely. Cold supper? I don't mention it. Here we go.

The image on my screen tips back and forth as Kristen positions her laptop on the coffee table in front of the couch, where Phoebe sits holding a notebook and pencil. This little girl, who has always had amazing stage presence, adjusts the screen, leans in close, and looks straight into the camera. "What is your name?" she asks with great seriousness, moving her pencil into place above the first line of the worksheet.

It's the simplest of questions. But I falter, uncertain how to answer. Kristen and her family are the only people in the world who call me "Dot," a nickname I despise on any lips but theirs, gained when baby Phoebe started saying it at the amazingly young age of eleven months. So now I'm Grandma Dot. But is that the name she's looking for here? Am I Dot? Or am I Dorothy? I explain my dilemma by setting one for her. Is she Pheeb, or is she Phoebe?

"Well," she says, "my family calls me 'Pheeb.' But at school— like on my homework, or on the board or something—I'm 'Phoebe.' I'm going to write down 'Dorothy.'" Good.

And on it goes. She has no idea that I was born in Texas, a fact that seems astounding to this child of Minnesota, marking me as an exotic specimen from a distant land. A little later, asked what work I do, I say, "Teacher." Close enough.

(In the background, Kristen says, "Dot, I hope you have a cocktail!" I ask her to call Mark on a different line and get him to bring me the glass of wine next to my dinner plate. I cannot step away from my post. Mark arrives with the wine, then leaves the room so he and Kristen can chat while my interview continues.)

Do I have brothers and sisters? Am I married? Yes and yes. I provide the details. Lots of spelling help is needed, but she hangs in there. I'm impressed by her stamina.

Then the plot thickens.

"Do you have children?" I pause.

What should I say? I have already been thinking about one of the questions I know is coming up: "What accomplishments make you proud?" Phoebe started to ask it earlier, but Kristen stopped her, pointing out that that question comes later. I have been planning to say, "I'm proud that I am a stepmother who is not wicked!" But that's not the question in front of me now. This question asks not about me but about my children.

Before I can speak, Phoebe is laughing into the face of the laptop, making eye contact across five hundred miles. "Of course you do!" she says. "You have three children: Kristen, Martha, and John. Duh." She speaks as if this is the most obvious thing in the world. These are names she knows how to spell. She adds them to her worksheet and moves on.

I move on too, on the surface, answering the rest of the questions one by one. But inside I am turning cartwheels and shouting with joy. "She didn't even have to think about it!" I silently exult. Phoebe didn't puzzle for even a moment over something that has aroused questions in me for most of my life. Her mother is one of my children. I am not surprised she comes to this conclusion. But I am overwhelmed to hear how matter-of-factly she declares it.

So this is who I am, or part of who I am. I call this part of myself "stepmother," which now, after many years, has expanded to include a "grand" as well. Phoebe knows that this is part of who I am too, even though she doesn't use the ugly word. Still, I hear in her voice the truth that I do indeed have a firm place in her life and the lives of her mother, brother, and father. Unlike the dreamed-of and zealously awaited place I have in the lives of the children born of my own body, this is not a place I planned for. But this is a real place, an important place, a place I embrace. It is a place others should not disdain.

Across the years, *stepmother* has become one of the words that help me understand the meaning and purpose of my life. It's not the only word that does that—*writer, friend, mother, wife,* and others are also important. But I know I'd be a different person today if *stepmother* were not on that list.

I've called this word *ugly*, as I believe it is for many people, but by now it also holds a certain beauty for me. That beauty looks like Kristen—after all, being *a* stepmother means, for me, being *her* stepmother. And that beauty also looks like stepmothers I have known, brave women who have taken up residence at the crossroads of loss and hope, offering love and care.

Few of us went looking for this role; in a sense, this role found us. But *role* isn't actually the best word for what we do. *Role* implies that there is a script with prescribed parts that could be filled by any number of actresses, and that's not quite right.

For me, a better word is *vocation*. Being a stepmother is not a role into which I was cast after turning out for auditions. It is a vocation into which I was called. It is a place of responsibility, located within a family and the larger society, where I am positioned to contribute to the well-being of others.

A vocation most often comes to a person within the give-and-take of relationship. Perhaps someone sees some special potential in you and offers you something to do. I first moved toward my vocation as a stepmother when Mark said "Marry me"—that is, when he loved me, chose me, and invited me to be his partner in life, which both of us by then understood would include helping him to fulfill his own vocation as Kristen's father. My first response to this call was to say *yes*, with joy. I soon learned that embracing this vocation would also plunge me into the depths—I had to struggle with fertility, hunger, scarcity, jealousy, and more. Now I see that responding to a call as big and important as this one is the work of a lifetime.

It has been clear at every point that my *yes* did not and could not stand on its own. My *yes* was entwined with the *yes* of others, starting with Mark's. Later, Kristen confirmed my call to stepmothering by allowing me to love and care for her, and by coming to love and care for me as well. My parents and in-laws confirmed my calling when they received Kristen and Mark and me into their homes as a family. Certain friends, the other parents in the Young Actors Shakespeare Workshop, and people at Holden accepted us too, confirming that our unexpected family had a concrete place in the social world. And Bekka acted with grace, honoring my legitimate place within the intricate structure of her daughter's life.

A vocation is not just something you feel. It's something you live out within a real world of relationships and institutions. The real world in which we live today includes millions of stepmothers, as well as millions of people—children and adults who have survived the loss of their original families—who need stepmothers who are strong and good, as everyone figures out how to live together well on the rapidly changing landscape of family life. I encourage women who take the risk of becoming stepmothers to proceed with care but also with hope. If we are honest about both the burdens and the blessings of this disdained vocation, we may grow in heart, mind, and soul, becoming who we are meant to be: People who speak the truth about the broken parts of our lives. Women who encounter the pain of others with honesty, courage, and compassion. Human beings who rest upon the earth, marveling at the meteor shower of grace.

Acknowledgments

This project began during a residency at the Collegeville Institute for Ecumenical and Cultural Research, where I had planned to write a wide-ranging book about how people may grow in wisdom and grace through life in community. I soon realized that my experience of the joys and struggles of this process came to a focus at one tender spot in my own life: being a stepmother.

Choosing to write about something so personal was frightening at first, but I've drawn courage from learning how many people are, have, or know a stepmother and how eager many are to discuss this disdained vocation. I've also relied on the support of generous colleagues and friends. In Collegeville writing workshops and subsequent conversations, Michael McGregor strengthened my writing and encouraged me to forge ahead through doubts and difficulties. Kathleen Cahalan and Don Ottenhoff provided abundant hospitality and wise counsel throughout the process. Bonnie Miller-McLemore, with whom I've shared conversations about every dimension of motherhood for decades, offered much-needed support and critique. Susan Sink, Barbara Melosh, and Kathleen Norris made important comments on early drafts, and excellent insights also came from Carla Durand, Laura Fanucci, Camilla Russell, James Nieman, and Christian Scharen. I am grateful for conversations in Valparaiso with Lenore Hoffman, Lorraine Brugh, and Agnes Howard and for comments from students and teachers in several classes at the Writer's Studio of the University of Chicago. I also appreciate the confidence in this book shown by Amy Ziettlow, agent Carol Mann, and Lil Copan of Broadleaf Books.

My greatest debts are to the three people to whom the book is dedicated—not because they helped me write the book (they didn't) but because they continue to help me live out the life and love the book commends.

Notes

Obtaining reliable statistics about how many stepmothers and other stepfamily members exist is difficult. In *Stepfamily Relationships: Development, Dynamics, and Interventions*, 2nd ed. (New York: Springer Science+Business Media, 2017), Lawrence Ganong and Marilyn Coleman, leading social researchers in this field, warn that it is very difficult to obtain accurate statistics on stepfamilies, largely because of how population surveys are conducted (7). For broad-brush quantitative information, I have relied on independent researchers who study families—notably, "A Portrait of Stepfamilies," Pew Research Center, January 13, 2011, https://www.pewresearch.org/social-trends/2011/01/13/a-portrait-of-stepfamilies/. Moreover, stepmothers are the least-studied members in this hard-to-study group; see Marilyn Coleman, Lawrence Ganong, and Mark Fine, "Reinvestigating Remarriage: Another Decade of Progress," *Journal of Marriage and Family* 62, no. 4 (November 2000): 1296–1307. Although stepmothers—and especially nonresidential stepmothers—are rarely the focus of family research, I did find many excellent studies, whose findings I will note throughout this book. I am grateful to the researchers and authors who have taken stepmothers seriously.

My first essay about being a stepmother—the one I showed to my stepdaughter and her mother a few years ago—was "Camping: Practical Wisdom in Everyday Life," in *Christian Practical Wisdom: What It Is, Why It Matters*, by Dorothy C. Bass, Kathleen A. Cahalan, Bonnie J. Miller-McLemore, James R. Nieman, and Christian B. Scharen (Grand Rapids, MI: Eerdmans, 2016), 64–87.

CHAPTER 2. ORIGINS

On marriage, divorce, suburbs, and housing in the postwar period, see Nancy F. Cott, *Public Vows: A History of Marriage and the Nation* (Cambridge, MA: Harvard University Press, 2000); Steven Mintz and Susan Kellogg, *Domestic Revolutions: A Social History of American Family Life* (New York: Free Press, 1988); and Eli J. Finkel, *The All-or-Nothing Marriage: How the Best Marriages Work* (New York: Dutton, 2017).

Cott confirms that the perception that only 50 percent of marriages would last—a dreaded topic of conversation among my peers at the time—was actually based on fact (*Public Vows*, 203).

On more stepfamilies formed after divorce than after death, see Ganong and Coleman, *Stepfamily Relationships*, 12. On the trend toward marriage as a class privilege, see Andrew Cherwin, "The Deinstitutionalization of American Marriage," *Journal of Marriage and Family* 66, no. 4 (November 2004): 855; and "New Census Data Show More Americans Are Tying the Knot, but Mostly It's the College-Educated," Pew Research Center, February 6, 2014, https://www.pewresearch.org/fact-tank/2014/02/06/new-census-data

-show-more-americans-are-tying-the-knot-but-mostly-its-the -college-educated/. Cherwin's article explores how changes in social organization and personal development have contributed to the growing prevalence and relevance of stepfamily arrangements ("Deinstitutionalization of American Marriage," 848–61). Sociologist Megan M. Sweeney, quoted on "unprecedented levels of voluntary partnership turnover," gathers research supporting this analysis in "Remarriage and Stepfamilies: Strategic Sites for Family Scholarship in the 21st Century," *Journal of Marriage and Family* 72, no. 3 (June 2010): 667–84.

Information on how people responded to questions of what their obligations are to various kinds of family members is from "A Portrait of Stepfamilies." Therapists who work with stepfamilies also report that the lack of clarity about roles and expectations presents stepparents with huge challenges; for example, see Patricia Hart, "On Becoming a Good Enough Stepmother," *Clinical Social Work Journal* 37, no. 2 (2009): 128–39; and Patricia L. Papernow, *Surviving and Thriving in Stepfamily Relationships: What Works and What Doesn't* (New York: Routledge, 2013). In addition, Amy Ziettlow and Naomi Cahn, *Homeward Bound: Modern Families, Elder Care, and Loss* (New York: Oxford, 2017), is an excellent study of how lacking expectations impacts stepfamily members at the end of life.

On the vulnerability of stepmothers to losing contact with children they have loved, two moving and beautifully written personal accounts are Julie Gosselin, "Nevermom," in *Telling Truths: Storying Motherhood*, ed. Sheena Wilson and Diana Davison (Bradford, ON: Demeter, 2014), 252–60; and Paula Carter, *No Relation* (New York: Black Lawrence, 2017).

Both social research and clinical reports observe that stepmothers have a particularly tough time; see, for example, Coleman, Ganong, and Fine, "Reinvestigating Remarriage," 1295–97; and Papernow, *Surviving and Thriving in Stepfamily Relationships*, 69. The "Dog Face" quotation is from E. Mavis Hetherington and John Kelly, *For Better or for Worse: Divorce Reconsidered* (New York: W. W. Norton, 2002), 193. Hetherington's study followed hundreds of families across a thirty-year period. The quoted passage continues: "Stepfathers rarely encountered this level of vitriol."

The film I discuss is Chris Columbus, dir., *Stepmom* (Culver City, CA: Sony Pictures, 1998). On Hollywood plots, see Hampus Hagman, "The New Mother: Replacement and Re-nuclearization in Hollywood's Narratives about Stepfamilies," *Film International* 11 (December 1, 2013): 6–12.

Chapter 3. Home

Elizabeth Marquardt's *Between Two Worlds: The Inner Lives of Children of Divorce* (New York: Three Rivers, 2005), is an important source for this chapter. The quotation is from p. 173.

Alison Clarke-Stewart and Cornelia Brentano, in their *Divorce: Causes and Consequences* (New Haven, CT: Yale University Press, 2006), survey several possible custodial and living arrangements but, noting the variety of circumstances, do not present a finding of what works best (198–212). Penelope Green's "Blending like the Brady Bunch? Let's Not Go Too Far," *New York Times*, November 17, 2010, describes a variety of living arrangements created by remarried couples who are reluctant to attempt the full "blending" of their families.

Delia Ephron's book is *Funny Sauce: Us, the Ex, the Ex's New Mate, the New Mate's Ex, and the Kids* (New York: Viking, 1986); the quotations are from pp. xiii, 158, and 161–62.

Kristen's last role in the Young Actors Shakespeare Workshop was Lady Macbeth, who cries "Out, damned spot!" in act 5, scene 1 of *Macbeth*.

The prophet urges the people to enlarge their tents in Isaiah 54:2. The quotation from Augustine is in his *Confessions*, II:7.

Chapter 4. Fertility

The Darwinian theories in this chapter are from Martin Daly and Margo Wilson, *The Truth about Cinderella: A Darwinian View of Parental Love* (New Haven, CT: Yale University Press, 1999), with quotations from 64, 8–10, and 10. On the increased likelihood of stepparental harm to children, see Grant T. Harris, N. Zoe Hilton, Marnie E. Rice, and Angela W. Eke, "Children Killed by Genetic Parents versus Stepparents," *Evolution and Human Behavior* 28 (2007): 85–95; and Greg A. Tooley, Mari Karakis, Mark Stokes, and Joan Ozanne-Smith, "Generalising the Cinderella Effect to Unintentional Childhood Fatalities," *Evolution and Human Behavior* 27 (2006): 224–30.

CHAPTER 5. THE UGLY WORD

On the origins of stepfamily words, see *The Oxford English Dictionary*. On orphans among Native Americans, see Marilyn Irvin Holt, *Indian Orphanages* (Lawrence: University Press of Kansas, 2001). On children in Europe, see John Boswell, *The Kindness of Strangers: The Abandonment of Children in Western Europe from Late Antiquity to the Renaissance* (New York: Pantheon, 1988). On England, its New England colonies, and the United States, see Lisa Wilson, *A History of Stepfamilies in Early America* (Chapel Hill: University of North Carolina Press, 2014), 13–14, 22, 47, 108, and 146.

For uses of the word *stepmother* as a metaphor for stinginess, see Immanuel Kant, "Groundwork of the Metaphysics of Morals," in *Practical Philosophy*, trans. Mary J. Gregor (Cambridge: Cambridge University Press, 1996), 50; Leo Tolstoy, *Anna Karenina*, trans. Richard Pevear and Larissa Volokhonsky (New York: Penguin, 2000), 684; and "Church Must Not Be a Stepmother and Must Not Send Faithful Away," *La Stampa*, May 16, 2015, https://www.lastampa.it/vatican-insider/en/2015/05/16/news/church-must-not-be-a-stepmother-and-must-not-send-faithful-away-1.35262563.

On language, see Barbara Melosh, *Strangers and Kin: The American Way of Adoption* (Cambridge, MA: Harvard University Press, 2002), vii, 2; Wednesday Martin, *Stepmonster: A New Look at Why Real Stepmothers Think, Feel, and Act the Way They Do* (Boston: Houghton Mifflin Harcourt, 2009), 222; and Barbara Waterman, *Birth of an Adoptive, Foster or Stepmother: Beyond Biological Mothering Attachments* (New York: Jessica Kingsley, 2003). Ganong and Coleman's survey of terms is in *Stepfamily Relationships*, 4. See also Kirsti Cole and Valerie R. Renegar, "The 'Wicked Stepmother'

Online: Maternal Identity and Personal Narrative in Social Media," in *Taking the Village Online: Mothers, Motherhood, and Social Media*, ed. Lorin Basden Arnold and BettyAnn Martin (Bradford, ON: Demeter, 2016), 39; and Judy Koenig Kellas, Cassandra LeClair-Underberg, and Emily Lamb Normand, "Stepfamily Address Terms: 'Sometimes They Mean Something and Sometimes They Don't,'" *Journal of Family Communication* 8, no. 4 (2008): 238–63.

"Blended" is widely used in the literature on stepfamilies—as, for example, throughout Trevor Crow Mullineaux and Maryann Karinch, *Blending Families: Merging Households with Kids 8–18* (Lanham, MD: Rowman & Littlefield, 2016)—but it often comes under criticism. Psychologist Patricia L. Papernow, perhaps the leading US expert on stepfamilies, reflects that "the expectation of blending has led all too many stepfamilies astray" (*Surviving and Thriving in Stepfamily Relationships*, 12). Two authors who pose strong objections to the term on the basis of their experience are Marquardt, *Between Two Worlds*; and Andrew Root, *The Children of Divorce: The Loss of Family as the Loss of Being* (Grand Rapids, MI: Baker Academic, 2010). Jesus's comment to his mother and his disciple is from John 19:26–27.

Maya Angelou, *Letter to My Daughter* (New York: Random House, 2008), xii; Cheryl Townsend Gilkes, "The Roles of Church and Community Mothers: Ambivalent American Sexism or Fragmented African Familyhood?," *Journal of Feminist Studies in Religion* 2, no. 1 (Spring 1986): 41–59; Deidre Hill Butler, "Other Mothers in Motion: Conceptualizing African American Stepmothers," in *Patricia Hill Collins: Reconceiving Motherhood*, ed. Kaila Adia Story (Bradford, ON: Demeter, 2014), 79; Linda M. Burton and Cecily R. Hardaway, "Low-Income Mothers as 'Othermothers' to Their

Romantic Partners' Children: Women's Coparenting in Multiple Partner Fertility Relationships," *Family Process* 51, no. 3 (September 2012): 343–59. On allomothers, see Sarah Blaffer Hrdy, *Mother Nature: A History of Mothers, Infants, and Natural Selection* (New York: Pantheon, 1999).

CHAPTER 6. HUNGER

My summary of "Hansel and Gretel" is based on the critical edition of Maria Tatar, *The Classic Fairy Tales: Texts, Criticism* (New York: W. W. Norton, 1999), 184–90. I also rely on Tatar for information about the Brothers Grimm and how the fairy tales they collected have been interpreted. See Maria Tatar, *The Hard Facts of the Grimms' Fairy Tales* (Princeton, NJ: Princeton University Press, 1987), 36–37. The quotations about children's fears of hunger and cannibalism are from Tatar, *Classic Fairy Tales*, 179; and Maria Tatar, *Off with Their Heads! Fairy Tales and the Culture of Childhood* (Princeton, NJ: Princeton University Press, 1992), 205. See also Jack Zipes, *The Original Folk and Fairy Tales of the Brothers Grimm*, complete 1st ed. (Princeton, NJ: Princeton University Press, 2014), xxxvii.

An intriguing blog post on why we compare babies and fetuses to food is Alex Van Buren, "I Just Want to Eat Her Up!," *New York Times Parenting*, May 19, 2019, https://www.nytimes.com/2020/04/13/parenting/baby/compare-babies-food.html. Van Buren's short essay incorporates insights from several cultures and academic research in a number of fields.

On how women in some cultures share care and food, see Hrdy, *Mother Nature*, 356–57; and Sarah Blaffer Hrdy, *Mothers and Others: The Evolutionary Origins of Mutual Understanding* (Cambridge, MA: Belknap Press, 2011), 73–82, 204.

On disparities after divorce, see Clarke-Stewart and Brentano, *Divorce*, 67–68 and 213–17. On added stress for stepmothers, see 228–29.

For a case of economic conflict between a stepmother and her stepchildren, see Wilson, *History of Stepfamilies*, 70–76. On conflict and cooperation about inheritance in stepfamilies today, see Ziettlow and Cahn, *Homeward Bound*, 128–35.

Julie Gosselin acknowledges her stepchildren's power to affirm or deny their relationship in "Nevermom," 255.

CHAPTER 7. SCARCITY

The story of King Solomon and the two mothers is in 1 Kings 3:10–28.

On stepmothers' difficulties with honored images of motherhood, see Caroline Sanner and Marilyn Coleman, "(Re)constructing Family Images: Stepmotherhood before Biological Motherhood," *Journal of Marriage and Family* 79, no. 5 (October 2017): 1462.

Hart, "On Becoming a Good Enough Stepmother," draws on influential psychoanalyst D. W. Winnicott's theory defining the "good enough mother."

The stepmother and mother who share some not-bad rules are Jean Blackstone-Ford and Sharyl Jupe, *Ex-Etiquette for Parents: Good Behavior after a Divorce or Separation* (Chicago: Chicago Review Press, 2004). The article by Jim Sollisch is "A Blended Family Survival Guide," *New York Times Motherlode* (blog), February 14, 2016, https://parenting.blogs.nytimes.com/2016/02/14/a-blended -family-survival-guide/.

Chapter 8. Jealousy

Jealousy as a theme in stepmothers' lives is reported in Elizabeth Church, "The Poisoned Apple: Stepmothers' Experience of Envy and Jealousy," *Journal of Feminist Family Therapy* 11, no. 3 (1999): 1–18. On triangles, see Hart, "On Becoming a Good Enough Stepmother," 131–32. Arielle Silver's very fine essay "Stepmothers: From Sinister Stereotype to Contemporary Counter-Narratives," *Lilith*, Summer 2016, https://www.lilith.org/articles/stepmothers -from-sinister-stereotype-to-contemporary-counter-narratives/, includes a story of her stepdaughter squeezing between Silver and the girl's father. I have heard similar stories from others.

Papernow's *Surviving and Thriving in Stepfamily Relationships* is an excellent study by an experienced clinical supervisor and therapist. The first of the five challenges Papernow urges stepfamilies to address is this: "Insider/Outsider Positions Are Intense and Stuck" (27).

In this chapter, I draw on two thoughtful and beautifully written personal essays—one by a mother, the other by a potential stepmother who breaks up with the child's father. They are Laura Lifshitz, "The Other Woman Who Snuggles My Daughter," *New York Times*, December 27, 2015, https://parenting.blogs.nytimes.com/2015/12/27/the-other-woman-who-snuggles-my-daughter/; and Sejal Shah, "Thank You," *Brevity*, no. 44 (Fall 2013), http://brevitymag.com/nonfiction/thank-you/. Shah's essay was later republished in her book *This Is One Way to Dance: Essays* (Athens: University of Georgia Press, 2020), 109–11.

Chapter 9. Mercy

Holden Village welcomes all to its remote location. Learn more about the village and how to visit it at http://www.holdenvillage.org. The psalm the women read under the starry sky is Psalm 148, as translated by the Evangelical Lutheran Church in America, in *Evangelical Lutheran Worship* (Minneapolis: Augsburg Fortress, 2006).

Paul's comments on love are in 1 Corinthians 13. On the early Christians' reconfiguration of family, see Lisa Sowle Cahill, *Family: A Christian Social Perspective* (Minneapolis: Fortress, 2000), 46. Among the sayings of Jesus that reflect a new understanding of family are Matthew 12:49–50 and Luke 9:59–60.

The song our choir sang is "You Are the Branches," by Michael Jothen (Choristers Guild, 1996). The words of the refrain are from John 15:5.

CHAPTER 10. VOCATION

In my own faith community, the idea of *vocation* provides a way of thinking about the places and relationships into which God calls us to love and serve our neighbors, from our family members to creation as a whole. *Vocation* is also used more widely, by people of other faiths or none, as they think about the meaning and purpose of their lives. Mark Schwehn and I have gathered a set of readings and offered some reflections on vocation in *Leading Lives That Matter: What We Should Do and Who We Should Be*, 2nd ed. (Grand Rapids, MI: Wm. B. Eerdmans, 2020).